D1645267

Winging It

Winging It

Twenty-one Extraordinary Interviews
from The Tommy Tiernan Show

SANDYCOVE

an imprint of

PENGUIN BOOKS

SANDYCOVE

UK | USA | Canada | Ireland | Australia
India | New Zealand | South Africa

Sandycove is part of the Penguin Random House group of companies
whose addresses can be found at global.penguinrandomhouse.com.

First published 2020
001

Copyright © Tommy Tiernan, 2020

The moral right of the author has been asserted

Set in 13.5/16 pt Garamond MT Std
Typeset by Jouve (UK), Milton Keynes
Printed and bound in Great Britain by Clays Ltd, Elcograf S.p.A.

A CIP catalogue record for this book is available from the British Library

ISBN: 978–1–844–88506–0

www.greenpenguin.co.uk

Penguin Random House is committed to a
sustainable future for our business, our readers
and our planet. This book is made from Forest
Stewardship Council® certified paper.

For the Tiernans of Athlone
My father Kevin
Uncles John and Brian
Aunties Emer, Maura and Mary

With lots of love

Tom

In memory of my Uncle Dan and Grandmother Mary

Contents

CONTENTS

Introduction

I can't remember what attracted me to the notion of doing an improvised chat show, but I do remember where I was when I got the idea. I was half drunk in a beige hotel.

Actually, I had two ideas that night. The other was for a sitcom about a detective who's looking for someone that may not exist. He has no photograph or description of the person that he's looking for; all he knows is that they're missing. He's hot on the trail of someone that he cannot describe. I thought it would make for a very funny existentialist comedy show – a cross between *Waiting for Godot* and *The Usual Suspects*. As yet, I've had no takers.

When I got the idea for the chat show I started laughing. And it's strange to recall that because the show, as it turned out, isn't really that funny. It's not comedy.

We've created a space where something is allowed to happen and we don't know what that something is until it's happening.

And whatever occurs, we give it the opportunity to develop. We have to – we don't have anything else to fall back on. Whatever we're talking about is all we have, and because there is no real structure to the conversation we can go funny then very sad and back to funny again. You know – like you would normally.

Heading into the unknown is always a risk and I get very anxious and hassled before each show. So bad at times that I wonder why I keep doing it. Am I addicted to stress or something? I've enough to be at without inflicting this on myself.

If you gave me the option of not doing the show each morning when we're working, I'd take you up on it. I'd much rather be walking around having unpressured conversations with people that I just bump into, or be at home in the garden smoking a pipe and listening to the birds.

But the feeling afterwards is the opposite – I feel transformed, as if I've been through something worthwhile. Perhaps you can't have one without the other. You have to be clenched before you feel the relief of release!

The guests have to be completely up for the stress/adventure of it as well. All I can do is try and settle their nerves by looking them dead in the eye and saying, 'Don't mind the audience, this is just me and you. Whatever happens, happens.'

Naturally, some of them never get beyond the rabbit-in-the-headlights state. I've been there myself on other TV shows so I wouldn't judge them too harshly for it. It happens when you have a particular version of yourself that you're trying to put across, that you're more used to putting across, and that you'd rather not deviate from.

This particular show is not the ideal vehicle for selling yourself as a 'personality' and the most interesting interviews, for me, are the ones where the guests aren't trying to do that.

For example, Brendan O'Carroll. It's a strange one for two comics to be on and not be trying to outdo each other in funniness. Speaking for myself, it's a huge relief when we're not, but the great fear comedians have is that when we're onstage or on telly we don't think that people will be interested in us if we're serious. We kind of feel that we're letting the side down and not doing our work. We get attention by being funny and, if we don't deliver, then what?

Every comedian that I know is as hilarious offstage as they are on, but they are other things too – smart, ambitious, thoughtful. Naturally rebellious. Brendan came on and wasn't trying to sell himself, and that's why it worked.

I was very nervous when Adam Clayton came on and then he said that he was nervous too. I suppose part of the technique of the show is to try and look for some common ground with the other person and to let curiosity be your guide, all the while aware that when somebody very famous is on, your curiosity mightn't be that interesting to them. You're only going to ask them questions that they've been asked a thousand times before. So you try and get beyond the fame and find common ground.

What in the name of God would I have in common with Adam?

Doubt, insecurity, hope.

This is what we have in common. And once we get talking about these things, we are, paradoxically, on solid ground.

Listening is the great challenge. I did a counselling course way back in the late 80s when I got a FÁS* placement with Galway Youth Services. We were asked to pair off with another person and do a little experiment. We were to talk while our partner, for the first two minutes, listened intently; for the second two, listened half on half off; and for the last two, didn't listen at all.

The general consensus in the group afterwards was that

* The state's training body that operated up to 2013 which had responsibility for assisting those seeking employment.

the first two minutes were the best. I was the only one who really enjoyed the last two minutes when the other person wasn't listening at all. I was fascinated to follow the thread of my own thoughts, and it is probably no great surprise then, really, that I became a stand-up comic.

Listening on the show is different. It's listening to let my curiosity go where it wants. And then it's about trust. Trust the question that comes into your head.

So, listening not forensically like a detective looking for clues – it's not a cross-examination. Listening in an attempt to be in the moment. That's the only technique, really, and even that makes it seem more formulaic than it actually is. It's a very casual affair.

When you're listening, you can't be doing anything else. You can't be simultaneously paying complete attention to your guest and also listening to your producer talking to you via a little earpiece that you're wearing, or referring to the list of questions that you've got written down on your cue cards. You have to focus totally on what they're saying and just hope that when they stop talking you'll have something to say.

And of course you do. And even if you don't, sure a little silence never hurt anyone.

Given the nature of the set-up, though – the nerves, the audience, the lights and the cameras, the sense of event – something will happen. There's too much energy in the room for us to fall into an abyss. It's atomically impossible for nothing to occur.

A lot of television is disheartening, but given the amount that has to be broadcast each day, that's not surprising. Five hundred channels going non-stop all year long – is it any wonder that most of it is banal?

I'm a horror to watch TV with because I spend most of the time shouting at it.

'Ah, Jaysus!'

'Bullshit!'

'For God's sake!'

I even have issues with the Angelus (it's too busy – just give me an unedited shot of a swan for a minute and it'd be grand).

It's so wonderful to hear from people how much they enjoy the show, but there's a danger in that too. If you get caught up in the success of it, you can't help but want to repeat it and there is a danger that you turn what people say about themselves into content, a commercial product. A revelation about trauma or pain becomes something that you exploit in order to make good television.

I hate doing television interviews myself. The freedom I feel on the radio disappears and the whole thing feels like more of a performance. Even when it goes well I feel like an imposter, that I'm putting on an act.

But I've never felt that way doing this show. I feel at home in it. No need to act the eejit, no need to be hopping about the place trying to have a 'stormer'. Just relax and chat and, if the funny comes, well and good, and if it doesn't, so what? Winging it might sound like something done on the fly. Instead, it's both intense and liberating, allowing things to take flight.

This was always the thing that I admired about David Letterman – his ability to be off-the-cuff funny. It's the real test of the comedian. Can you come up with something on the spot that is as good as anything that you might have written?

When you're performing something night after night, a

piece that maybe you thought of six months previously, you're really more of an actor than a comedian. You're an actor playing the part of a comedian; it takes time and craft to perfect a story, and it works.

But at a gig the biggest laughs of the night often come from something unplanned – a heckle and your response, an unexpected thought, a reaction to something. This is what attracted me to the idea of the chat show. The freshness of it. You think of something funny and you say it and move on. You're not repeating it night after night for the next eighteen months.

I'm curious about the possibilities of conversation, the interrogation of the moment – what comes up. It excites me.

What are we, these two people right here, right now, aware of?

What is the nature of it?

Can we have fun with it?

Is it serious?

Can we speak honestly to one another?

And also the physiological effect that words can have. I remember years ago doing some sort of experimental therapy where the psychologist was trying to put me in a trance. His method was to get me to repeat sentences that he'd come up with and for me to let him know when I felt that I had gone into some sort of altered state.

Now, these are subtle changes – not like taking acid, but still real. The ones that worked were to do with the reality of the situation that we were in, ones that were honest. For example, he'd get me to repeat something like: *'I'm here because I want you to heal me.'*

And I'd feel the hairs on the back of my neck stand up and

a numb buzz envelop my head. Then, from this changed perspective of mine, we'd talk.

It sounds a bit daft in hindsight, but all I can say is that it happened and that I remember coming up with stuff that I didn't know that I knew – a wisdom that was in me that I couldn't normally access.

I've felt the power of the spoken word onstage doing stand-up where the audience and I are all slightly high at the same time. You wouldn't be sure how you got there and all you can do is enjoy it.

The same thing has happened on the TV show. Someone says something or is sitting in front of you singing and everything changes. It happened when Christy Dignam stood up and sang 'Ave Maria'. Impossible to explain; all you can say is that you were altered.

Wonderful moments – wonderful even when we are speaking of pain.

I can't claim much credit for the success of the show because I'm only a bit-part player in it. I don't choose the guests and I don't think that it would be good if I did and had a load of questions prepared beforehand. That, for me, would be the route to lifelessness. I'd be impersonating somebody, acting the way that I thought a chat-show host should act, trying to be responsible and professional. To this day, I still can't say, 'Join us after the break,' without feeling like a fake.

The types of conversation that we have on the show are possible for anyone, anywhere, at any time, with anyone. All we have to do is be open to it. Not easily done, but no great adventure is. The adventure of encounter and intimacy – that in our lives we can talk openly with one another without fear of burdening.

9

Maybe doing three conversations in a row each night is a bit much. After the conversation with Bob Geldof I didn't really come back to myself until halfway during the next guest. The great thing about Bob – apart from his natural eloquence and instinct for voltage – is his openness. Whatever came up, he just went with it as honestly as he possibly could. Joe Brolly is the same. They use words as creatively as a composer uses notes.

And when someone is speaking about grief, like Bob did, you share the space with them. We spoke for nearly an hour and then I went straight into another conversation with someone else. I should have gone for a short walk to re-gather my senses.

Other interviews are effortless in a different way. I probably had the most fun talking with Aoife McLysaght. She's a college professor and we just had good craic yapping about evolution, DNA and other things I don't really understand. She tolerated my ignorance very generously.

I've screwed up a few times, for sure. I haven't included any examples in the book, but one interview that comes to mind is when I met the comedian and mental-health activist Ruby Wax. I was trying too hard to be God-knows-what and we went off piste for a while. She was on a book tour pro-moting something that she'd been working on for a few years. A kind of self-help manual about emotional aware-ness. What I meant to communicate to her was my fear of finding out why I do things because then I'd have to address them. But whatever way I said this, she took it as a dismissal of her book and she was rightly pissed off. I'm sorry that it went that way, but I do remember thinking at the time that this was probably making for good TV. But I didn't go looking for that tension and I wouldn't like to be the type of host that would.

The easiest interviews, in a sense, are the ones where I don't know the guest at all. Rather than be struck dumb wondering how the hell I'm going to talk to this stranger for forty minutes, I'm actually quite intrigued from the get-go. I know that they're on because they have a story to tell and all I have to ask them is 'Who are you?', and they're off. The most important thing here is time. Give them the time to speak freely. The interview isn't an audition; they don't have to impress me. I'm a naturally curious person and all it is is a chat.

When the idea came up to put some of the interviews into a book, I said yes immediately. The difficulty was choosing them. We could have gone for twenty-one other interviews and the result would have been just as good.

The twenty-one conversations here are from across the four seasons of the show. They have had a minimal amount of editing – just to knock out repetition and smooth out any confusing bits – and they include some material that didn't make the broadcast because of the length of the show.

Reading them again brings me back to the freshness of the original encounters. Not only have they lost nothing by being put into print, but they have gained resonance. It's all there on the page – finding the common ground (or sometimes missing it), trying to connect, listening. The cogs and wheels of honest conversation. Truth be told, I prefer them this way. And in the quiet of a book the power of what was spoken is permanent and clear.

Adam Clayton

'I feel like I've got friends all over the world. There is nothing quite like being able to bump into someone, absolute strangers that you don't know, and they tell you the most intimate things about themselves. This is the only job where that happens.'

Tommy: The most obvious question to ask a bass player is: 'What do *you* do?'

Adam Clayton: I'm a little nervous tonight but at least *I* know who I am.

T: You're just off the road.

AC: Since November, yeah. In fact, we were in the 3Arena and we were hoping you might come along, so . . .

T: Yeah, there was awful traffic getting out of Galway that night! I wasn't able to make it . . . When do ye need to tour again? Or do ye ever need to tour?

AC: You mean like that kind of itch that needs to be scratched? It'll be when we make a record, when you're excited about the songs. It's when we kind of get fed up of being around each other for a year or so whenever we're making a record, and we feel like we've got some songs to go back out on the road with. And when you feel you're wanted. Sometimes you don't want to go out there when people feel you've only just gone away.

T: Is there a lot of pressure in being in U2 in terms of trying to be popular?

AC: Not any more. For me, it's amazing that we've had – don't tell anyone – forty years of being in this band. We grew up in Dublin, had these dreams about making records, touring the world, and that was just for one album. And now it's fourteen or fifteen albums and we're still doing it. Utter gratitude, you know? I feel like I've got friends all over the world. There is nothing quite like being able to bump into someone, absolute strangers that you don't know, and they tell you the most intimate things about themselves. This is the only job where that happens. [*To Tommy*] It happens to you – I'm sure you meet people and you hear these amazing things. Sometimes it's what your songs or your work has done for people, or it's just stuff they tell you. And that's hard to give up. I wouldn't want to give that up.

T: I'd be a massive fan of the band, but there's also a lot of things I'm very curious about. I suppose everybody in Ireland probably has an opinion on U2. Can you tell me how the money has changed you? I'm always fascinated by this. Most Irish people think we've grown up in the same kind of social class. And it's not something that people are prepared to talk about very much, if they didn't come from money and their life suddenly changes. What's your relationship with money? Is it a tension in your life?

AC: When you experience success on that level – financial success and career success – an adjustment has to take place. And I'm not sure if we've always dealt with it as well as we can. It's allowed us to live amazing lives. It's allowed us to experience amazing things. But it's also allowed us to pursue an obsessive-compulsive pursuit of music. You can't take it for granted. I mean, every time you make a record, every time you go on tour, there is jeopardy. It's not like U2 is a Heinz baked-beans tin and you just churn out more. You have to create ten songs and you have to believe that other people want to hear them and then come and see the show. So there is a high degree of risk in what you do. So you always have this strange relationship with the success. We've been very lucky because we've been able to do great things with it. One of the things we're most proud of is the Music Generation initiative that the Irish government and ourselves have been able to achieve here in Ireland.

T: Tell me about that.

AC: We met this amazing woman called Rosaleen Molloy, who told us there was very little funding for music classes for children in school. She had this vision of how you could roll out free tuition for kids across the country. We had to start small because it was based on how much money you could put into it. Gradually, we got two or three counties, and it's been rolled out to the point where the government has stepped up and is putting the extra money into the programme. It's stuff like that, where you see children from all around the country that didn't have access to tuition expressing themselves through music and having access to music. In some ways, more than anything else that's the proudest achievement for the band and myself. Absolutely.

T: What lengths do you have to go to as artists to find the place where the original new music comes from? *The Unforgettable Fire* is such an important album to me. It seemed to me at that stage you were taking chances. There was something very strange going on with that album that seemed to work. It was incoherently coherent, and it spoke of spirit. I'm just a little curious how you access that creativity, what you have to do. And are you prepared to pay the price each time to do it?

AC: I think it's not worth it if you don't do that. For me, each record is like a progress report of how far you've come in your life. And at times it's really hard to go in there, to play the bass or do another take of that song, because you just don't know where it's going. But you have to trust in the process that eventually you'll get to a place where it means something to you. And if it means something to you, there's a chance it'll mean something to the people listening. Music is a mystical thing. You can't dial it in. A song like 'One', if you were a musicologist and examined why that works, you'd say, 'It doesn't have quite the right structure,' etcetera, but it had *something*, that thing that you mention. The songs on *The Unforgettable Fire*, one of my favourite records, they have that *something*. There's an inarticulateness to it that just allows the spirit to soar. We are part intellect, part spirit and part physical, and music seems to water the spiritual part of us.

T: But is there a sense that you put yourselves under an awful lot of pressure to be 'successful', to be 'relevant', and that sometimes that desire for commercial success can put too much pressure on the adventure? Trying to be successful is a very different adventure to trying to explore.

AC: Well, yeah, we're not part of a knitting circle! You're trying to work in an area where being successful is one aspect of it. You want to have some kind of a cultural connection. If you write songs that people don't hear, then it's not really very satisfying. U2 has been through various different cycles. I don't know what the next cycle is going to be. Maybe being successful or 'commercial' in that sense is going to be less important to us. Art and commerce – there's always a little bit of a rub, and I think we've come through it pretty well, actually. When we put out songs like 'With or Without You', at the time they were not obvious songs that the radio was going to play. So we do tend to try to walk that line of connecting, but also things that are fresh to your ear. That is part of the challenge. It's the difference between fine art and commercial art, I guess.

T: It's wonderful to hear you speak! You don't often [get a word in edgeways] . . .

AC: Well it's great to be here on my own!

T: I'm getting a very strong sense of Leonard Cohen off you.

AC: That'll be the hair . . . but I think I'm taller!

T: But just a sense of calm and gentleness and manners.

AC: I wasn't always like that. I was a brat. I couldn't wait to get out of school quick enough. I think you and I have similar experiences there – we were in boarding schools. I hated it. The world was too small for me. I was incredibly lucky because I left this somewhat removed boarding school and met these three amazing guys in Mount Temple Comprehensive. My first term there, I thought, I'm going to be beaten up, I'm the guy arriving in the middle of the year, I come from Malahide, I've got a posh accent – they're going to hate me! I'm just going to try and get on with everybody and make myself stand out a little bit. And I didn't get beaten up too much.

I met these three guys. They were interested in forming a band. And it turned out one of them was a great singer, one of them was a great guitar player, and one of them was a great drummer. So we took on the world. Back in 1976 in Dublin, it was a dark, grim city. The pirate radio was just beginning to make it seem interesting. It was the three-day week, it was the petrol crisis. There wasn't a lot going on for you if you were seventeen or eighteen, so we threw ourselves into the band.

Because I didn't have any academic ability, I became the manager – briefly! We eventually found Paul McGuinness and he became the real manager, and we just worked really hard, but we worked really hard at what we believed in, which was that music could be 'our thing'. We looked about going to the UK, and we thought, no, we don't really fit in there. We sort of leapfrogged that and focused on America, and we found that Americans were actually quite nice people, and they had this great music tradition, and they liked Irish people. And it grew from that.

To go back to your original question, success very much went to my head. By the time we were twenty-five and twenty-six, we could pay our rent no problem, we owned cars, we could travel. And by the time *The Joshua Tree* hit, we could buy houses. Now, anyone I've met that has experienced success and fame in that way and in those years, it takes them a long time to recover from it. You lose your sense of yourself. I was very unhappy so I drank and drugged and got myself in tabloid newspapers and embarrassed everyone I knew and myself. But you come through it, you learn from it. And maybe that's what young men do anyway. But I also realize that to want to do this, you've got to be a little bit different in the head, and I find that even though drink was the main problem for me, I still have to really work quite hard at keeping my sanity on and off the road. My thinking can take me to bad places, it's not always reliable. And it's great having three other guys who can check you sometimes, and we check each other.

T: How does that manifest itself, that kind of . . . *dark* energy is the wrong word, but that kind of vulnerable, structureless mood?

AC: It's just the internal talk that happens. It seems to me that addiction manifests itself in many different ways. Partly it's your family of origin, what happened there, whether you were nurtured or whatever. And partly it's whether you had a childhood trauma, and that doesn't necessarily have to be losing a family member, it can be a number of different things, separation from parents, etcetera. So once you have that in your DNA – where you feel restless, questioning, irritable, you're not sure what to believe – it's really hard to undo that programming. That's what I went out into the world with.

T: Does time onstage give you a break from that?

AC: Yeah. That two hours onstage when we're performing is great because I know exactly what I'm doing and why I'm there and I don't question it. I don't have time to think about it. It's that old cliché: being totally in the moment. And also you're doing it with these three men that you've known for a long time, and they know you. So that is again going back to where we came into this. That is the most amazing thrill and the most amazing reward, to be able to perform concerts. Nowadays I feel like U2 are just the reason why people gather. Once people gather, something else happens. There's an event or a party and we're just the warm-up for that.

T: When you're performing in front of such huge crowds – fifty, a hundred thousand people – do you ever feel slightly anonymous up there? That you're the source of all this energy but you're removed from others at the same time?

AC: I watched the Queen film [*Bohemian Rhapsody*] the other night and I was really reminded of the utter loneliness that you can feel, particularly on those tours in America before mobile phones, where you drive for six or eight hours, you'd be let out of the bus and on to a stage and there'd be however many thousand people all thinking you're brilliant. Then you go back on the bus and you go back to a hotel room on your own and you go, 'What do I do today?' That's

a loneliness that very few people experience or will understand. And I'm very happy to say that doesn't happen any
more. I'm extremely happy to be in a hotel room on my own
these days.

T: Could you give me a description of a day in your life
when you're on the road?

AC: These days it's just about discipline. Being able to get
through the day. I wish it was more exciting. I don't sleep late
any more. That's the great thing about alcohol, you could
always sleep late. No, I'm up sometimes eight or nine, even
after doing a gig. I'll start the day gently, looking at a few
emails, and if we're in America, then I try to make some
phone calls home – I got married a couple of years ago and
we have a young child. So I try and have some interaction
with her. And then I'll go to the gym because I'm a bit of a
runner. I stopped smoking about twenty years ago. I always
imagined I was going to die a smoker, but I did manage to
give up cigarettes and now I'm grateful for the breath that I
have. Then you get ready for soundcheck.

T: Does a plane come and collect you?

AC: Yes, Tommy.

T: I have to drive myself to Ballinasloe! Yes, I mean, I'm
sure it gets old, but it sounds exciting to the rest of us.

T: So with no pressure for a next album or a next tour, do
you play a lot to keep musically active?

AC: I have to confess I'm not very good at picking up the
bass. Have you ever played bass on your own? It's not a lot of
fun. It's *dum-dum-dum*, five minutes on this note, then that
note. I wish I was more of a virtuoso. I wish that was my
background and my training because that was all I ever
wanted when I would listen to the bass players I was excited

about, to be one of them. But I haven't managed to achieve it. But I think what I have managed to achieve is that I'm probably the best bass player for U2. And, you know, I'm happy with that. I quite like the mistakes because in the mistakes that I make sometimes I go into new territory.

T: Could you tell us about some of the famous people that you've met.

AC: Early on I realized that famous people and the work that they do are two separate things. And there are famous people like Leonard Cohen where you just want to be in their presence because you want that 'blessing'. But most of the time I respect what somebody does, I respect the music or the film or painting or whatever, but I'm not rushing around trying to get a selfie with someone. Bob Dylan is another one of those people where it feels like a blessing. I mean that's a man who's won the Nobel Prize for Literature. He invented a whole way of writing. He elevated folk song into music as commentator, music as journalism for what's happening. So I'm very grateful to him.

T: I get a sense of a kindness off you.

AC: Thank you, I'll take that.

T: Because you come across to be so sincere, it makes the times when you've gone off the rails seem all the more authentic. I met a guy once who played bass instead of you at a gig in Australia. He's living in Connemara now.

AC: That's Stuart. We still have a relationship. I don't hold it against him. He doesn't hold it against me.

T: Could you tell us about that? Maybe people aren't familiar with what happened.

AC: I don't mind going there. I think talking about it helps me get rid of it because it was an utterly humiliating moment for me. I had realized that I had an issue with alcohol and I

had what we professional alcoholics call in the business 'cold-turkeyed' and 'white-knuckled' not drinking. I'd been doing really well. We were going to be filming the show. The night before, I thought I might have a glass of wine. We were in Australia and they do great wine there. So I had a glass of wine, and then another. I don't know what happened after that, but about three days later I woke up. I had not turned up for a gig in a stadium that was being filmed, that had a lot of money resting on it. I had let the guys down, the three guys who stood by me since the age of sixteen. I'd let down the audience and the road crew. It was not a great place to be.

If ever there was a moment of realization where you wake up and go, 'I have a problem and it's bigger than me and I need some help,' that was it. And, you know, it arm-wrestled me to the ground. I could have lost everything at that point, but the good news is that, actually, people did forgive me. I took responsibility for my issues. I'd love to say it was plain sailing from that point on, but it really wasn't. I'm really glad I came through it. I'm really glad I'm here and able to talk to you about it, because the alternative would have been a lot worse.

T: You have to be able to [admit] though, even though it was a high-pressure situation with a lot of jeopardy in it, it's great to arrive at a place where you can say it was OK and forgive yourself, rather than punishing yourself for something that happened thirty years ago.

AC: I guess, for me, learning is how you get over these things. You know, perfection is a great thing to seek, but I don't think it exists. It's how we deal with the imperfections, how we get over them, how we deal with the failures in relationships. That's the real struggle.

Aoife McLysaght

'We keep refining what we know. Every day; you hope to be a little less wrong than you were before.'

Tommy: So what do you do?

Aoife McLysaght: I was thinking about this coming in! Do your producers hate you? I'm a professor in genetics in Trinity College Dublin. Also, I suppose I was trying to think, why did they ask me? I did a thing called the Royal Institution Christmas Lectures on BBC Four recently. These are science lectures that have been going for nearly two hundred years.

T: What were you lecturing about?

AM: Evolutionary genetics. So the title of the lectures is 'Who Am I?'. So we explored this through all of evolution. We started out the three lectures so the first one was, well, who are you? Well, you're an animal, like any other animal. And we were exploring the similarities we see between us and all the other animals, and trying to make people see again, you know, that you're part of nature, you're not something special. You're special to yourself, but not in terms of . . .

T: But we are *miraculous* . . .

AM: Well, that's one way of looking at it.

T: Aren't we?

AM: Well, it depends on what you mean by 'miraculous'.

T: I mean the fact that we're here and that we're conscious of being here.

AM: Every life would be miraculous to me, but we're not especially miraculous. If there's anything special about us, it's that we can think and do things like science to help us understand where we came from and recognize those relationships with all the other animals.

T: And we can laugh, and have sadness and joy, and we're aware of it . . .

AM: But we're not the only ones with sadness and joy. So this is what we were trying to say, to reinforce the idea that we are part of nature, not separate from nature. We were looking at human origins, and also how you're not any old human, you're *you*. Everybody is unique.

T: Why did they ask you to do the lecture?

AM: Yeah, I don't quite know. You're still trying to figure out why I'm here! I've done various bits of public communication of science over the years and I do lectures and talks and little bits of radio and things from time to time. The first person they asked was Professor Alice Roberts, who does lots of telly. She's a medic who does anthropology and anatomy and all these kinds of things. I know Alice from various work things and she said she'd do them if I did them with her. She was very nice and brought me in on it.

T: Through your study of genetics and evolution, what have you learned?

AM: That's a hard one . . . thanks for that! So much stuff . . . I've learned how much I *don't* know. Maybe that's a characteristic of scientists in general, that you become aware and actually comfortable with the fact that you don't know everything. People always expect scientists to know everything and have opinions on everything and be informed, but actually, part of being a scientist is understanding that you don't know every-thing and that you're just trying to figure it out. The stuff I try to figure out is looking at DNA sequences and comparing them. So if you compare the DNA sequences of everybody in this room, you can quite quickly see the relationships. Some people might have very close relationships, some people in here might be siblings, but other people will have relation-ships that are a bit more distant. We can actually see that every human is very, very closely related – we are a really young species.

T: I'm dizzy already. Go back a bit . . . DNA – what is it?

AM: It's a chemical in every cell in your body that carries the instructions for building you. Our genes are all made of the DNA. When you take a single cell which is just a ferti-lized egg that will grow into a human or chimpanzee or a dog, the thing that makes them grow into a dog or a human or a chimpanzee is the DNA they contain.

T: OK. Could you mix them?

AM: It probably would just not work.

T: Well, I didn't work for a long time! Do you mean *on the dole* 'not work', or just wouldn't be born?

AM: Probably not be born. You can to a degree, and that's when people create hybrids with artificial breeding, but if things are too far apart in evolutionary terms, it just won't work.

T: Did I read something stupid that we're also like bananas or something?

AM: We share DNA with bananas, yes! Actually, every living thing on this planet shares DNA. Every single thing.

T: Does that suggest to you that we all came from the same source?

AM: Yes, it does. Definitively.

T: How can it be definitive if it hasn't been proven?

AM: What proof do you want, other than the fact that we share this DNA? The only place you get your DNA is from your parents. There's no other way to get DNA. The same is true for bacteria. They get their DNA from their 'parents', for want of a better word. So if you have DNA that's shared between us and bacteria, it's because way, way back when, we shared a great-, great-, great-, great- – add in twenty minutes of that – grandparent.

T: So can you imagine a single source for the billions of different life forms on this particular planet?

AM: Yes.

T: That's amazing, isn't it?

AM: Yeah, it is, it's totally bonkers. It's quite amazing.

T: So there was some type of 'protospasm' . . . Are you impressed with that word?

AM: Lovely!

T: I'm not entirely sure what it means, but I think it might be a sexual thing, but anyway. There was a single single-cell amoebic life . . .

AM: An amoeba is even a bit more advanced, actually.

T: I'm getting ahead of myself. Pre-amoebic. And what caused the diversity to happen?

AM: We don't really know for sure. Complex things like us have lots and lots of cells that make up a big body. Plants are also complex; there's lots and lots of cells in them. And then you've got simple things that are only one cell big, like bacteria, for example. Our brain is the most complex thing that's ever evolved and we still don't understand it fully. But it turns out that one thing that was really, really important is this single event which was kind of peculiar. Basically, all things looked like bacteria at one time in the world, and one of them was eaten by another one, which happens all the time, but it stayed alive inside it. And that's the origins of all complex life. So the bacteria that stayed alive inside the other bacteria-like cell is now called mitochondria, which you might have heard about if you did science in school.

T: I failed science. I just . . . my brain isn't good with science in terms of facts. I'm much more in tune with imaginative stuff.

AM: But, you see, that's I think a misconception about science, that it's not imaginative or creative. To work in science and be a scientist, you do have to be imaginative as well.

T: It's like people who can play the piano and build one. You can do that. I can't – I can just about play the piano. I don't have the facility to build one. So these single-cell things, was there originally just one to begin with on the planet?

AM: There was probably never a time when there was one cell but there would have been a population of them. But only one of them is our ancestor, you see. The other ones would have died out.

T: So it wasn't unusual for cells to go around eating cells?

AM: No, it was food.

T: The cell that stayed alive inside the other cell. That was unusual, was it?

AM: It's not totally unheard of. It's happened a couple of times, but only a few times in the history of all life – which is a few billion years!

T: So from that live cell being inside the other cell that had eaten it – what happened then?

AM: We don't really know, but probably the main thing is that this changed the energy dynamics so the cell was now a bit more independent and could grow into bigger things.

T: Which cell?

AM: They now are one thing. So if you look in any cell with a microscope, any cell in your body, you're going to see mitochondria inside. We don't call it a cell any more because now it's just a part of our complex cells, but it was originally a free-living cell.

T: So what happened then? When did we get shops?!

AM: We don't really understand – or at least I don't – the transition from single cells, even ones starting to get a bit more complex, into big multicellular organisms. We can kind of see some steps like you do see with bacteria, when they can sense each other's presence. But there's a big difference between sensing that other cells are around to becoming a multicellular organism where it feels like you're just one thing and not a collection of cells.

T: So the growth of all that is miraculous, isn't it? Us being alive here and experiencing one another, now, on this planet. That's not logical. That doesn't make sense. That's not a rational event. It's full of rationality but there is something – even if it's only my imagination talking – something stupendous about being alive, isn't there?

AM: There is, absolutely. But when you're trying to say it's miraculous and not rational or logical, I think it can be both. It is miraculous. Life is amazing. In terms of genetics, the more I know about the process of development, where the fertilized egg grows into a little baby, that is so damn amazing. It seems incredible that it could possibly work. So I do find it miraculous but I think there also are explanations to be found.

T: Do you think that there are dangerous days ahead for our species in terms of overpopulation?

AM: Yes. And climate change. It's not being taken seriously by lots of people. I don't have special expertise in those things, but it does seem to me that some form of life will survive, but we want to be among those things. I think overpopulation and climate change probably go together in certain respects because the wasteful things we do that use up far too much energy and make too much pollution are multiplied by however many billions of us there are. If it was a small number of people doing that kind of thing, it wouldn't have so big an impact. But the things that used to be OK when we were a smaller population aren't OK any more.

T: There's a great American comedian called Bill Hicks . . .

AM: I *love* Bill Hicks.

T: He had a great line – he said that human beings were basically a virus with shoes. Looking at what we do to the Earth, do you get a sense that we act in the same way that a virus does, in that it sucks up everything that it needs for its own survival from its environment, irrespective of the damage it causes, until that environment is a wasteland?

AM: Some people do. Some people are very conscious of it. But I think it's almost back to what you were saying earlier about what makes us special – we are capable of understanding this, and we're capable of changing our actions. We don't have to be like that. So there's actually, maybe, room for hope.

T: And looking back at the evolution of all species, we have this story in our minds about times when every living thing had been wiped out during an ice age, and then stuff slowly starts to grow again. When you're looking back at DNA sequencing and stuff like that, do you ever come across evidence that it's actually part of some kind of natural process?

AM: So, with the Ice Age, it wouldn't be that all life on the planet was wiped out, but it would have been wiped out from areas. But what you do see is that there's a huge crash in diversity – some species would have gone extinct, but then other things wouldn't have. After the ice melted, certain things would have moved back into those areas. One of the things you can do with DNA is you can trace the geography of the DNA variation, so you can retrace patterns and paths of migration.

T: Isn't that kind of incredible that loads of things become extinct and there's a great shrinking, and that the life force within the Earth never loses the ability to spring out again in a million different directions? That's fantastic.

AM: The other big extinction, of course, is the non-avian dinosaurs. Everyone knows that all the big dinosaurs went extinct. The only ones left are birds – they're dinosaurs as well. They were totally dominating the planet and the only mammals that were contemporaries of those probably looked like little rodents or something along that size. It was only after the dinosaurs went mostly extinct that there was this opportunity for the mammals to spread out and take all these different niches.

T: With the similarity between people's DNA, it seems to me that racism is the daftest thing in a modern country.

AM: Absolutely the daftest thing. Absolutely we are all so closely related to each other and so, you know, we have differences. You and I have differences between each other, everybody in this room has differences between each other. There's all kinds of differences, but the fact that people hang up on a few superficial differences – and skin colour is *very* superficial – it couldn't be more superficial than skin colour. And so it's just a difference you can see.

T: I think it's important to hate people if they vote Fine Gael or support Chelsea, but other than that . . .

AM: I don't know about football, but I know about politics, so I'll go [with that]!

T: Looking forward then, I know you can't predict, but are there things that you can see, 'If all these things have happened and if that continues to happen, what's ahead of us is *this*'? Are you able to see down the line?

AM: Yeah, you mean for our species?

T: Yes, for life.

AM: We can't predict the future in terms of evolution, but one thing we do see with our species, and it's part of why racism is kind of a nonsense, is we've been really constantly mixing. So what we see today and the things that look like what people think are our big fixed differences today, it's just one snapshot on a constantly mixing thing. And so we can anticipate that we'll keep mixing like this and so we'll just keep changing. It's like somebody is stirring a big cake mix or something!

T: A big pot of people.

AM: Yeah, a big pot of people being mixed, yeah! And so that's what we can expect, and maybe now, I suppose, it probably happens faster than it used to because transport is so much faster and people can move around the globe. But even without modern transport, what we see from looking at genes and looking at the DNA is that our species has been mixing the whole time, and we all come from Africa originally.

T: Whereabouts?

AM: The Rift Valley is where it is considered to be. That's where most of the fossils are found. But we know this because of those patterns of genetic diversity and retracing those paths of migration back to Africa.

T: But aren't there always surprises? Like, the whole news cycle of scientific research is surprise. Anytime you buy a copy of *Scientific American*, it's always, 'We thought we knew this but actually we know nothing.'

AM: I suppose you're right, but it's not that we know nothing, it's that we keep refining what we know. Every day, you hope to be a little bit less wrong than you were before. That's it. One of the big surprises that did come up in relatively recent years is that we also include Neanderthals in our recent family tree now, as a kind of archaic human.

T: They're from Slane.

AM: Is this a Navan/Slane thing?

T: I went to school with some of them, I swear to God. They didn't get further than the Inter Cert, but they played football and they were very violent.

AM: They should have been playing rugby then, they were wasted in football!

T: There was no rugby then in Navan back in the day.

AM: But this is an interesting thing that was discovered when they sequenced the Neanderthal genome. You find the bones and you can get the DNA out of it. When compared to a modern human genome, you discover that we actually share lots of DNA with Neanderthals, and the only way you share DNA is if you inherit it.

T: But would people not have a general sense that we came from Neanderthals anyway?

AM: No, so Neanderthals and modern humans were contemporaries – they met and had fun together! Why did they die out? Well, there were probably fewer of them. Another idea is that they might have been more pacifist, but I don't know if there's good evidence for that. But, in a certain way, they didn't die out because we just blended together so well. So maybe the way we are today is partly because we have these natural ancestors.

T: I watched the documentary recently about seven or eight different scientists, and one was, like, a microbiologist, and there was some sort of space person, and they both said that we actually know very little. There was a report recently where the top linguistic professors in the world – Noam Chomsky was one of them – they all said, 'OK, the game is up. We have to tell the people, even though we're getting paid, that we actually have no idea where language came from.'

AM: Yeah.

T: Isn't that phenomenal?

AM: It's amazing that people think about it deeply enough to realize what you don't understand. But a lot of it's the same. If we talk about the human genome, for example, it's about 3 billion letters long. We write it as letters in shorthand for the different bits in the sequence, but only about 2 per cent of that looks like genes. The rest, we don't have any idea about.

T: Isn't that fucking fantastic, then? We're walking mysteries.

AM: It is the best! So that's the kind of thing that I find interesting. If you're doing science, it's because you want to figure things out, not because it's a section of the library that you just go and study. What you want is questions that you don't know the answer to. It's fun trying to figure out things. One of my favourite little facts is that while only 2 per cent of our genomes looks like genes, there's 8 per cent – four times as much – that is the leftovers from an ancient viral infection. When you get infected by a virus, what it does is it injects itself into your cells. If you get infected by a bacteria, it's just in your bloodstream but it's not inside your cells.

T: So if someone opens a tomb and some sort of fly comes out from Tutankhamen and bites them on the face, they can get a virus that could wipe out the whole world in ten minutes?

AM: Yeah . . . perhaps!

T: I saw that in a movie.

AM: I'm sure it was *really* accurate! But 8 per cent of our DNA is virus DNA left over from it. So, in a certain way, you're more virus, you could say. Bill Hicks was more right than he realized.

Blindboy Boatclub

*'The bag allows me to express things that a human
doesn't. I'm a cartoon character, I'm like Homer Simpson.
I don't have to account for things the way a normal
human with a face would.'*

Tommy: Now ... what the fuck are we going to talk
about?

Blindboy Boatclub: My sports commentary, man.

T: What??

BB: I'm Marty Morrissey.

T: You've the cut of him, all right.

BB: I do, yeah.

T: What are you up to?

BB: I just wrote a book ... [*BB is interrupted by a sound-man
adjusting the microphone*] Ah, I knew it now, the rustling of the
bag in the microphone. I've a bag-rustling problem.

T: It's weird because I was only just thinking about you.
The last few times I've seen you on TV, I've been blown
away by your passion and intelligence. You're on fire.

BB: Thank you very much.

T: You've stuff to be giving out about, don't you?

BB: I've a fair few things to be giving out about, yeah. I
try my best, like. What I've found is that I'm a clown, like.
I'm a fucking clown.

T: You're very angry for a clown, though.

BB: Yeah, but clowns are allowed to be angry. The things that I say are not in any way remarkable. It's just, because I look like an ape-shit, people listen. People are used to people in suits saying certain things, so you need to change the delivery of the medium and then all of a sudden people pay attention. Like Trump is doing it the opposite way, you know?

T: Dressed like a suit, but talking like a clown?

BB: Yeah.

T: Do you've a degree in something?

BB: I've a few different things. I did a Masters last year in socially engaged art, which is a way of bringing art out of galleries and into the public sphere, because art is gone up its own hole. I studied psychology as well for years. I studied psychotherapy because I've a massive interest in mental health, so why not bring that into what I'm doing.

T: You've amazing passion – you're concerned about the country.

BB: Absolutely. Being from Limerick, it has got the highest rate of suicide in the country. Limerick is technically still in recession. Limerick got a fair wallop off the recession and it was mainly people my own age [who suffered]. The recession would have hit when I was in my early twenties. Half my friends went to Australia and the other half died. And the ones that didn't die were left with severe mental health issues because of the lack of support systems and the pressures of their daily life and the lack of seeing a future. So I just found myself looking at my Facebook and Twitter and seeing that 70 per cent of men under thirty in the country follow us online, so I was, like, how can I bring some of the stuff I learned training to be a psychotherapist to those people, but do it with a medium that isn't intimidating, do it with a bag on my head, do it through a bit of craic. One of the things with mental health, you don't have to be solemn to be serious. The metaphor that I use sometimes is, if someone breaks their leg, what happens is you call around to your mates and everyone will sign your cast. It's a way to deal with an injury. Wouldn't that be lovely if someone said, 'I've got anxiety, I've got depression' . . . sign their head cast or something. Or, I don't know, sign their thoughts.

T: Is what you do fuelled by anger about the way things are?

BB: It's not really, it's driven more by a sense of duty, of just, if people are already listening to me, younger people, and the government aren't giving out the tools to help, what can I do to make their lives a little bit better? What words can I speak that might let me connect with them, make them feel that stuff isn't as hopeless? . . . Again, I used to suffer from anxiety and depression and stuff like that, and I came out the other side of it using psychological tools. I wouldn't mind people learning a bit about that because a lot of it you can get through self-help.

T: Like what?

BB: Cognitive behavioural therapy – that worked for me. If you have anxiety or depression, you retrain how you think and that means you won't experience unpleasurable emotions. So we're not taught that in school. We're taught fucking religion. We're taught at the age of seven, 'Go in there to that upright coffin and talk to a stranger and tell him your secrets. And then he'll tell a magical guy in the sky to sort it out for you.' That's not a way to sort out any issues. We learn this shit when we're kids. I'd rather see kids learn emotional intelligence, CBT or mindfulness. Instead of learning about haunted bread.

T: It sounds hard going, continuously watching yourself and keeping an eye on yourself.

BB: Maintaining my mental health? It's no different to maintaining physical health. Every single day I would use these tools.

T: And if you don't do that?

BB: Then I'm back to square one. If someone was unhealthy, smoking a load of fags, eating take-away, not exercising – if they sort their shit out, in six months' time they'll be healthy. But if they go back on a bad lifestyle, they'll find themselves in an unhealthy position again. After ten years of being free from anxiety and depression, I would be a depressed and anxious man quite soon if I didn't use my tools and allowed myself to fall back into negative patterns of thinking.

T: It sounds like you have a lot of care, then, for people who are in that situation.

BB: Because I was able to come out of that and it wasn't even as difficult as I thought it would have been. I was in a hopeless place, but because I came out of it, I'm going, 'Jesus Christ, why isn't this in schools? Why isn't this available to everyone, these tools?'

T: Can you describe the hopelessness to me?

BB: Can I describe the hopelessness? My thing was anxiety and agoraphobia, so I was afraid to leave the house as a result of anxiety. Then because of that I got intense shame. The shame then led to depression, so I had anxiety and depression living as best friends. I was unable to remember a time that I was happy and I was unable to imagine a time that I'd be happy again. I was able to get out of it because I was in college and counselling was free. If you're not in college or if your parents can't afford eighty quid a week for counselling, then you're fucked, and that's one of the issues with this country. The best mental health services in the country are charities, unfortunately, people like Pieta House. That shouldn't be the case. You should be able to go to your GP and the GP goes 'There's a counsellor now and that's on your medical card. There's no six-month waiting list, you can get that next week.' That's the service that should exist. And then to prevent that proactively, kids from about three years up should be taught basic psychological tools to understand and be resilient with emotional stress, which we're not taught. And the reason – and this is bordering into conspiracy theory – we're not given these tools in Western society in general is because we can't be advertised to if we're completely mentally healthy. When was the last time you saw an ad for a bar of soap where they're telling you how clean it will get you? They don't tell you how clean it will get you, they show you a picture of beautiful people. They're trying to sell you a better version of yourself, but that only works in a population that is not emotionally aware. When someone becomes emotionally aware of how they're feeling, then they start buying soap for how clean it gets them. They're not going to be sold this ideal version of themselves because they're grounded enough to know 'That soap is not going to make me a better person.' Capitalism relies upon populations that aren't too self-aware. That's just conspiracy theory there, that's just me smoking too many joints.

T: Can you talk me through discovering Blindboy, and what that felt like to be alone and sad and not enjoying life, and after a process over a while, suddenly finding, 'Jesus, there's freedom in this and there's a platform.'

BB: Well, ironically, one of my issues was social anxiety, so it took putting a bag on my head to feel comfortable speaking to a room full of people. But mainly I use the bag for my own privacy. I'm conscious of the fact that I just want to go to Aldi and buy toilet roll and not have people talk to me about 'Horse Outside'. The bag allows me to express things that a human doesn't. I'm a cartoon character, I'm like Homer Simpson. I don't have to account for things the way a normal human with a face would.

T: Freedom.

BB: Freedom, yeah.

T: You've beautiful eyes.

BB: Thank you very much, Tommy. Thank you.

T: No, you do! I'm struck by the level of care you have for people.

BB: Again, there is a level of selfishness to it. This is a part of my own self-awareness. The reason I do this and try to help other people is because it helps me sleep better at night. I go to bed at night thinking I did something to help some-one today. If we give a fiver to a homeless person, it is an act to help that person but, ultimately, it makes us feel good about ourselves. It doesn't make the act selfish, but I think it's important for us to be aware that there's a kind of hedon-ism to it. But a responsible hedonism, a compassionate hedonism. Otherwise, I can go up my own hole if I think I'm only doing this for other people. Part of my journey in men-tal health is having self-compassion and compassion for other people.

T: Do you worry about falling back? Do you sometimes feel like you're on thin ice in terms of being healthy?

BB: I don't know about that. The tools that I have are very strong, so I can spot triggers in my thinking and behav-iour in advance and stop myself. I can question my thoughts. If I see myself allowing anxiety or sadness to take over, I can spot it very early. With CBT, what you do is you treat your thoughts like you're a scientist. So if I start to say to myself, 'I'm a bad person' or 'I'm a piece of shit,' what CBT would teach me to do is to write that out on a piece of paper and say, 'Where in my life is the evidence that I am a piece of shit?' And by looking at that, I'd go, 'Well, there's actually no evidence whatsoever.' That's the rational approach for looking at these toxic thoughts that lead to toxic emotions that lead to falling into depression or anxiety. So that's what CBT does for me. It doesn't work for everybody. It just happened to work for me. It's one of many schools of psychology that are out there for people.

T: What are you like without the bag?

BB: Do you know what, I'm the same as I am now. I'm not too far off. I mean, the character that I have has grown a lot over the years, but I'm a lot closer now to who I actually am. I just have the bag for privacy, like I said.

T: There's great wisdom in your mask, for sure . . . So if I met you without the mask, you'd be a slightly calmer version of this?

BB: I'd be the exact same. I just wouldn't have a bag on my head.

T: You've beautiful eyes and a beautiful smile – I'm starting to sound like a weird priest – but honestly, you do!

BB: Thank you, thank you!

T: In terms of The Rubberbandits, workwise, what are ye at?

BB: At the moment, I just wrote a book, fifteen short stories called *The Gospel According to Blindboy,* because it's fiction and gospels are fiction. You'd enjoy it, actually, because you're a fan of Flann [O'Brien], aren't you?

T: Totally.

BB: I'm obsessed. Flann O'Brien was the person who turned me on to comedy – not comedy, but the Irish way of comedic thinking. So the book that I wrote would be very heavily influenced by Flann. I can't get away from him. He's there in my creative heart, and James Joyce as well. You'd like it. There's a story in it about Éamon de Valera, an alternative history, where he has an immaculate womb like Holy Mary, except in his bowels, and Michael Collins has to get him pregnant so he can give birth to these warriors out of his arse that will free Ireland. It's good craic.

T: I can see it now – the *Book at Bedtime* on RTÉ! But you're right, Flann O'Brien is the godfather of us all. He's phenomenal. And are you gigging still?

BB: Still doing gigs, yeah. We might head over to London for a while. I've a podcast now as well, *The Blindboy Podcast*. We're just arsing around doing the usual thing. People always ask me how are we getting on. We've been going for seventeen years. Our career trajectory can only be described as ah-sure-you-know-yourself-tipping-away. That's our career.

T: I think everybody who works in Ireland, that's their career.

BB: Yeah, sure you know yourself, tipping away.

T: I remember one time I was over in London and I went for a stroll around the Southbank. It was my dream to go and see the Globe Theatre. They reconstructed it as it would have been four hundred years ago, with the exact dimensions and everything, to perform Shakespeare and give people a real feel to how it would have been. I took a stroll down there and I saw this poster: 'Live tomorrow night: The Rubberbandits.' Phenomenal.

BB: We were the first ever entertainment act to play Shakespeare's Globe. But the Brits have a totally different attitude to us. They have us like 'high art' or something, it's weird. Over here, we're just clowns, but over there it's, like, 'Oh, they're doing something very clever now.' I think they think we're the IRA. I'm not sure.

T: I suppose they have to work at something now that the war is over!

BB: Yeah! 'Just put them into a gallery now, they won't blow nothing up.'

T: Are the Bandits gigs angry and funny?

BB: Absolutely. We try and do a bit of a punk-rock thing in that respect. The subject of our songs always touches on social things but we just do it in a ridiculous fashion. The arty-farty in me is pure inspired by these lads called Dada. Did you ever hear of them? Marcel Duchamp in 1916, he put a toilet into a gallery and called it art. But the reason was because he was looking at what was happening in the First World War and saying, 'The world is so irrational.' The ir-rationality of machines shooting down people was so insane that the only response that art could have was to put a jacks into a gallery. 'The rules are out now – what are we going to do?' And that's Dada. I've always found that hugely inspiring – to be faced with something that is so painful that you have to find a toilet and put it into a gallery. For me, it's putting a fucking plastic bag on my head, being a clown on television and people listening.

Bob Geldof

'Grief reduces the soul to an atom. But that's not
the issue. The issue is that you learn, and I'm lucky
'cause I do music . . .'

Tommy: You're getting better-looking as you get older.

Bob Geldof: That's just because you were born forty years after I was.

T: You always have great clothes.

BG: It's a leather jacket and jeans, eh, Tommy . . .

T: Anytime I see you being photographed and stuff, I'm always kind of struck by your [style] . . .

BG: Yeah, you could do with a bit of . . .

T: . . . A bit of fixing up. We think we know stuff about you. Is that a burden to you, that we think we know you?

BG: No, because, not so much a conscious decision very early on, I was never interested in the star thing. I wanted the fame thing, but I wanted that so you'd have a platform to talk about the things that bothered you. I still feel I can't do the red carpet with any grace, I just rush past. I feel embarrassed being in a limousine, though when it all started happening, where they'd send limousines for you and there was your old Volkswagen or getting the limousine . . . The only way I thought that you could stop that happening was by just talking on shows like this about the stuff that happened to you and just talking openly. And I thought then, if there isn't this sort of spurious mystery that accrues around people, if there's none of that, if you are what you see, then that won't become burdensome to you. And I think that was largely successful in some areas. And then, in other ways, it became a problem in itself. But by and large, I think generally people have a fix – it's one way or the other; he's an idiot or he's OK. And both of those things are true simultaneously.

T: To me it's more that – and I don't know if you were worried about this just as a place you didn't want to go – I suppose sorrow travels in front of you in terms of our awareness of your story.

BG: Yeah, I know that's true too. But it's balanced again by . . . I've described this life as being bizarrely episodic, and it's like you're in your own – I hope this doesn't sound grand, because I really don't mean it to be – it's like you're in your own soap opera and you find yourself in the middle of a scene that in no way have you constructed, but you're there and you're in the middle of it and it's unfolding. And like anyone's life, there's not much you can do about it. And that episode seems to stop and then become another episode. So it really is tiring.

Obviously, incredible things have happened to me and there's been the karmic downside, though I never believe in the karmic ragtag and bobtail, but it's so present and obvious. People know the highs that have happened to me or they've been involved in, you know, making The Boomtown Rats huge, which they were involved in because they bought all the records and cheered us on, especially in this country. And then, you know, the downsides of that are the family and the downsides are Live Aid, and it's all extremely public, but that's the nature of my life and job so there's no use coming on your show and saying, 'I'm not going to talk about that.' That's bollocks. So you do it and that means you can get on the bus or you could walk down the street.

I think I've talked about this, so forgive me, it became so impossible directly after Live Aid that older ladies in particular would come up to me and just stare, and they'd reach to touch you and break down in tears. And this was disgusting, you know? So you had to escape from that and go back to what you do, which was play music and be a pop singer. You know, it got confused about who I was and what I was doing. Not to me, you know, but that's it. It's precisely the same exactly with your kids – a pain in the arse or you thrill in their glories or you take them through the next bit. You're all the time like this, the parental radar is whizzing constantly, no matter what age they are, that doesn't stop, as every person here watching in the audience knows.

T: I suppose because every parent has their worst nightmare, it seems amazing to us that when we see people who have lived through that, that they're still walking.

BG: Last week, I went to the funeral of my mate's son, and he didn't want me to come for fear that I had to relive it, but I had to be there for him because it is . . . unbearable. And no, you don't . . . No . . . Time doesn't heal, time accommodates. And it's ever-present. You're driving along and you're at the traffic lights, and for no reason whatsoever, the person in question inhabits you and I'll cry. And then I look around to make sure the people next door don't see me or aren't taking a photo and posting it or something. But that happens to everyone. And so you say, 'OK, it's time to cry now,' and you just do it to the maximum because there's no use holding it in, lights are green, or whatever you do before, and then you go. That will always be there and you accommodate that. But it's not coherently there. It seems to me like

46

you can't put a boundary around it once you understand the nature of this because it is boundless and it is bottomless. The grief and the abyss is infinite.

T: The grief is bigger than you are.

BG: Of course it is! I mean, of course it is! If you've ever stood in a desert, you understand how the great psychedelic religions, these sort of vast imaginings of a god, Islam or Christianity or Judaism, of course they come out of these vast empty spaces where you are nothing. I've stood in the Sahara, in the middle, under these vast skies, and these infinite sands are the middle of an ocean, and you're standing there going, 'I'm an ant.'

Grief reduces the soul to an atom. But that's not the issue. The issue is that you learn, and I'm lucky 'cause I do music, and I'm not trying to steer this around to the fact that The Boomtown Rats have a new album! But I am lucky because Phil Davidson, who's a novelist friend of mine from Dublin, he says he writes books to put a frame of reference around that which he's experienced, and that's correct. That's brilliant. And so I get to write songs, not consciously, like, 'Now I'm going to write about Peaches, now I've got to write about Paula, now I'm going to write about my wife, who gives me boundless joy.' I'm not going to do that because that's too obvious, but you do. I can spot it in the songs now. I may not be aware, but it puts a frame of reference. It says, 'No, it's not boundless, Bob. You can contain it.' It's like a USB stick and I find an available slot in my headspace and I put it in there, and every now and again at the traffic lights, it slips out and I can hold it in front of me, like, literally almost, and I go, 'I know you, you fucker, get back in there,' and I can slot it back. And it's there and it's shimmering away all the time.

But then it's probably affected me less, if you can say that, than the rest of the family, or her sisters or her daughters. It's just been lived openly, and this life has happened to a lot of people, and it happens in extraordinary circumstances in my case, which is why I just get tired of the soap-opera nature. I mean, it's so extreme. The things that happened . . . just stop! Stop!

T: I don't know if you've read *The End of the Affair* by Graham Greene . . .

BG: I love *The End of the Affair.*

T: When the character asks God to leave him alone. He says, 'I'll leave you alone if you leave me alone,' because of what he has been through. He doesn't want any more.

BG: I don't have that luxury, because there is no God so I can't go to him. I just rail at the fates, not that there are any, you just do that. I find myself onstage with the band sometimes just literally going like that [*shakes fist at sky*]. And that's because I'm in excelsis. I'm not being sober Bob, I'm Bobby Boomtown then and I'm away with the fairies. You can do and say anything. That's where the drug is. That's why you want to go out on a stage. And just when that band makes that racket, that absolutely excites me and I'm gone. And that is the catharsis. I leave the stage and I'm utterly exhausted emotionally, psychologically, physically, but alive. Alive. Do you mind me being terribly name-droppy?

T: No.

BG: So I was with Bruce Springsteen last week, and I don't know if you read his book [*Born to Run*], but it's spectacularly good. For me, arguably better than the songs. The guy's a writer, and he's got the Irish thing The Rats have. They've just made a two-hour film about The Rats [*Citizens of Boomtown*] and Charles Shaar Murray, the great critic from the *NME* and Jimi Hendrix biographer, was talking about The Rats' songs and he says, 'It's a specific Irish thing. It only happens with the Irish and rock and roll. It's Van, it's Phil Lynott, it's Springsteen, and Geldof can do it.'

Bruce tells great stories, but he has this terrible depression. Real bad. I was talking about it and saying, 'Do you not think that these manic four hours onstage, is it that because, when you leave, you know that maybe you're going to go back to that massive crash which happens periodically?' And he said, 'I don't know.' He said it comes and goes. You probably get it. Performers go on and on about it. But it bears on your earlier question – I think I need [performing] for that reason, where I'm rooted, bizarrely, and where things seem to make a different sense, but a coherent sense.

T: Are you surprised that you still have an audience for the music?

BG: I'm surprised if there *is* an audience for the music!

T: How old are you?

BG: I'm sixty-eight. No, I'm not [surprised]. It's a great band, you know.

T: Who turns up at the gigs?

BG: So if you take the Isle of Wight festival,* there was a hundred thousand people. So there'll be a bunch of them who know the band from the 70s and 80s, and they'd be mouthing along the words. And you can see their children, fifteen, sixteen, and they're giving it large, and you think, OK, great. And it would seem like an exercise in nostalgia, were it not for the fact that I made six solo albums after The Rats sort of came to a logical end after Self-Aid.† It was ten

---

* The Boomtown Rats played a reunion show at the 2013 Isle of Wight Festival.
† Self-Aid was a 1986 benefit concert for the unemployed in Dublin.

years, and in those ten years, these kids from Dún Laoghaire, they needed to invent their own lives. There was nothing going on in Ireland in the mid-70s, nothing. And so they had to change their own lives and they set about doing that, and as they went, they helped to change the country a bit. Then they helped to change music a bit and then they helped to change the world a little bit. Then they stopped.

T: So, say you're in the 70s, in your mind, who are you aping? What star are you following in terms of 'I want to do stuff like they're doing'?

BG: It didn't turn out like that. It turned out like any bunch of kids who get together – I like this, and I like that, and I like the other. But by the first rehearsal where we were all, like, you know, it was just a laugh, we understood that we just couldn't do a bit of this, a bit of Bowie, a bit of that, it just wouldn't work. So what we all had in common was early 60s rhythm and blues and mod music – The Who, The Kinks, The Rolling Stones. And because of them, a reference back to Muddy Waters, the blues, Lightnin' Hopkins, Howlin' Wolf, Dylan, Woody Guthrie. People forget that about The Boomtown Rats – we took our name from Woody Guthrie. I came across the name in his biography – he was in a gang when he was a kid called the Boomtown Rats.

So we came with clear intent and purpose and we chose the music we all had in common, which was rhythm and blues, but we wanted to play it very fast. And one afternoon I was at a friend's house in Sandycove and he played me a new album by a new band called Dr Feelgood, and he played me an album by somebody who I had never heard of called Bob Marley and the Wailers. And I just said, that's the North Star, that's what we had to be doing, what the Feelgoods had done. By 1975, rock 'n' roll had clogged itself up with pomposity. The Rolling Stones were much more about the length of their limousines or the width of their mansions than they were about music, and it was all grim. Dr Feelgood stripped it back to four-tracks and they wrote a very aggressive rhythm and blues, but songs about where they came from in Canvey Island. And I listened to the lyrics, and Wilko Johnson was writing about the oil flares on the gantries in Canvey Island in Southend. And so when The Rats arrived in London, we all made a pilgrimage there.

And then I listened to Bob Marley and I could not understand what he was doing. What is this, calypso or what, but with a band as natural as Van Morrison's greatest bands, as natural as Willie Nelson's bands, as natural as The Band. And I listened to the lyrics and I remember listening, and he's just messing with words and making sounds. And I took both the albums back to the lads for the rehearsal that night and we just listened to the Feelgoods, instantly got it, learned it off. And then we tried to get our head around reggae.

For the documentary, Kieran Fitzpatrick gave me a load of little cassette tapes he'd made of us in Gardiner Street and in the Cliff Castle in Dalkey, and we're playing 'Get Up, Stand Up' or 'Stir It Up' or something. And no one knew what it was. So that's how we started and that was where we were going. And I think we lived up to it, you know. 'Looking after Number One' is still played, and I wrote it in the dole queue in Dún Laoghaire, and I wrote 'the world owes me a living' on my dole card. There was a queue. It was that pitiless November sting of a rain and it was past nine, and there was these lads of forty, through no fault of their own, unemployed. Ireland, 1975 or '76 – forget it. And a lad in front was reading the *Racing Post*, and he had a pencil in his ear and I tapped and said, 'Can I borrow it?', so I wrote. It was supposed to open at nine. There they were inside, in their cozy little civil service with the stove on and drinking tea. Meanwhile, everyone was freezing outside. It was nine fifteen, I wrote: 'The world owes me a living, I've been waiting in this dole queue too long, I'd been standing in the rain for fifteen minutes, that's a quarter of an hour too long.'

And I sing it now in the wake of the catastrophe of 2008, where countries were humiliated, tens of thousands committed suicide, where no one went to jail, where the shysters are still in control and where we elect the same fools to perpetrate the same carnage across the world. Where wars resulted from the crash, where migrants resulted from the wars where we block our borders to stop them, where we leave the unions that have given us peace for seventy years, and Brexit, and I just couldn't stand it any more.

When Garry and Simon* came to me and said, 'Do you want to get back and do the Isle of Wight?' Yes, because I wanted to hear the noise that wrote 'Rat Trap' about homelessness. When Zuckerberg and Google and Apple and your phone and your television are watching you all the time, when CCTV is watching you, when Europe is now debating whether to allow facial-recognition cameras everywhere, I can sing 'Someone's Looking at You' with the same conviction. I can sing 'I Don't Like Mondays' because, two weeks ago, there was another massacre. It's not yesterday, it's now, and I will sing it with the same rage and animus and I'm not going to stop.

And one last thing – I will sing 'Banana Republic', but this time not for here, because we grew up, but towards the American Republic, because God knows what happened to

* Garry Roberts and Simon Crowe, fellow members of The Boomtown Rats.

them. I did sing it there four weeks ago at a gig in the Beacon Theater, and I dedicated it to that vulgar fool in the White House. I think they got it.

T: Am I naïve then . . .

    BG: Yes.

    T: . . . to pray. And am I naïve to believe that if the heart has a hunger, it's because that food is there somewhere, a hunger for communion, for oneness? Is that an idiocy, do you think?

    BG: Not at all. It's glorious. It's essentially human. And though I'm an atheist, if you pass a hurt person and you see it, as opposed to in your busy life where you're rushing past, but you acknowledge it and you walk on, then you are complicit in the misery. That's me, that's my voice, and to recognize it and do nothing, something essentially human withers and dies. The most that most people can do is put a euro into the Concern box or the Oxfam box or whatever. And what they're in fact saying is, 'Dude, let me give you a hand-up there.' When a million people do that, it's political, and then the ball starts to roll. And that's why I always go for that endgame, because you can keep giving that homeless person a quid, knowing it'll get them a cup of coffee or the next fix or something, but a million people do it and the government starts to get a bit nervous about stuff. And if you can gather that sense of 'No, I don't like this, I made my gesture and it cost me a euro, I'm a bit bothered by this,' then that's really powerful.

So your point about 'Am I naïve to pray?' Not at all. All people pray, but they're praying to anything. It's the higher-power thing, though I don't believe in a higher power. I had to answer some questionnaire thing for *Mojo* magazine last week and they said, 'What happens after death?' And I said,

'Blessed oblivion. *Basta*. Gone. I got through that one.' And that's what I hope. I will be very disappointed if there's something afterwards.

T: Even if it's nice?

BG: Yeah. I mean, I was in the Scouts and, back in the day, there were three flights out of Dublin – Manchester, London and Lourdes. I was eleven and we went to Lourdes, and it's burned in my memory. I really didn't believe the stuff then either, is the truth. We had to be dipped in the filthy water, and I didn't like that either. But what's in my mind is late night, the torchlight processions, which for me looked like hundreds of thousands of people holding their little flames. And it was not the people who were ill, it was the people taking care of them who I really did notice, and said, 'How do you do that?' You know, how can you just be that person's mouth, arms, legs? That struck me, and that still strikes me. So, you know, your question is the question everybody asks – should you pray? Yeah. Should you be silly to believe that it'll come true? No. But there's an even chance that whatever you're praying for will work out.

T: Can I ask you what happens to you when you talk?

BG: I try and tell you what I'm feeling. I don't really think about it that much. Why?

T: Because it seems anytime I listen to you talk, you're so fluent and creative, and I just wonder, do you have those feelings of creativity and a world that you're creating when you talk? So you're taking all these experiences and all these things that you notice, and when you get on a roll, it's like you're redefining the world. Do you delight in talking? Do you love talking?

BG: That's the Irish thing. I mean, it really is. We have the words, and I've often said that in the UK – 'I'm Irish, you know, we have the words.' It is a thing we do. It's absolutely part of the game here. It may be less as everyone disappears into, you know, cyber-nothing, but when we were children, we didn't have TV and stuff. And my dad would come home on Friday, he'd be away all week working, and it was difficult trying to establish a relationship with his three children again. It's boring. I didn't have a mum, so it was difficult to try and get a family vibe happening. And at seven or eight o'clock on a Friday night, he would do the cooking because he used to be a chef before he was a traveller, and it was always good the food at the weekend, and it would kind of be silent. We'd just kind of be embarrassed, like this awkward semi-stranger who I didn't love, I feared and had angst with – we both ended up loving each other, of course, but you know, boy–dad thing – so I was being grumpy and sullen, and the oul fella would sit there. He didn't actually say this, so I don't want someone tweeting like crazy, I'm just trying to think of an example how he'd do stuff; he'd put down his knife and fork, and he'd go, 'All the same, that fella Hitler had a couple of good ideas'! You know? Something so manifestly outrageous! Of course, all hell would break loose around the table.

Roy Foster, the Irish historian, he was a friend of my sister, and so he'd be there, and he's written about this like it was like some Beckett play. The old man would referee it – you had to make your point, impassioned as it might be. When I got to thirteen or fourteen, I was [passionate], and my sister Lynn is the same, and my elder sister was sort of the conservative one.

T: I'm trying to find the thread there.

BG: Conversation was nurtured, it was organized, it was structured. You won the teatime round, sort of, if you could argue the others into submission. Sometimes Lynn would get so worked up she'd cry with passion and then I'd win, so the thing was to get her so wound up. Yeah . . . Very weird.

T: Where did the Geldofs come from?

BG: I'm Belgian Catholic, English Jewish, German Protestant, Irish nothing. I got the Irish nothing!

T: Tell us about what The Rats are up to over the next while and tell us the name of the album.

BG: We had a single out a couple of days ago, which is mega, the two-hour documentary, that new album, *Citizens of Boomtown*. Faber asked me could they do the collected lyrics for forty years, which was flattering, so that's called *Tales of Boomtown Glory*. I don't think any of us knew that we were in a great band. We're in a great band. It just kicks off. And I don't care. I cared when I was a kid – I was worried that The Clash were selling faster than us, that the Sex Pistols record was better than us, and we need a new record and all that stuff. Couldn't care less now – it's just straight-on rock 'n' roll. And I don't think I'd come on this show and big-up a record if I wasn't convinced. Well, I love this record. The noise . . . Someone needs to sing these blues, the blues of the now. And it doesn't do it for me, some twenty-six-year-old geezer with a guitar, it just isn't enough. There has to be some visceral thing that spits in the eye of the present. And if that's these old geezers from Dún Laoghaire, County Dublin, Ireland, so be it. And that's where I'm at.

T: Two more things I'd love to ask you.

BG: Go on.

T: Talk to me about sex.

BG: *'Well now, Tommy, how often do you do it a week!?'*

T: Well, what I mean is, I'm fifty. I want to know what sex is like when you're sixty-eight.

BG: Difficult. Um, I mean, you know, thank fuck the tyr-
anny of sex ebbs. You're not completely in its grip. That
laser-driven drive of a sixteen-year-old clearly isn't there.
And as you age, it tempers, which *you* must understand at
fifty. And then, by sixty-eight, it doesn't always need chemical assistance, but it fucking helps. And also, you must be
very careful, because the beauty of a long-married wife hides
in plain sight, and you must always look to that woman who
animates you so that once again she electrifies you.

It's very easy with my missus, who I've been with for
twenty-five years. I'm sort of a one-woman geezer. And I'm
not being soppy here, but being happy together is such a
turn-on, that you're sitting there watching the box – and I'm
really fucking annoying, I've got the remote here and the
guitar here and the knees are jiggling – but when I'm not
doing that and we're there . . . When Paula left me and it
became almost impossible to live and I was kept going by
some close friends, Pete Briquette from The Rats being one
of them, I remember a futile flight home from some thing in
Europe, and I was going back to nothing because my home,
my family, everyone I'd loved, and this edifice I'd constructed, 'Bob World' – because it hadn't happened here as a
kid, as I've explained, so I set about constructing a family –
all that had gone. And I really didn't understand why I'd lost
everything I took to be true. And I was on this plane back to
nothing, and I was saying, 'Why am I even flying, why don't
you stay and go anywhere, because they've gone?' And it was
so disorientating and discombobulating. 'Sad' just doesn't do
it. I'm sitting in the plane and there was this couple bickering
non-stop. And he got stuck into a book and she was reading
a mag. Ten minutes to landing, everyone starts doing the
belt, and as the wheels came down, she just put out her hand

and he covered it. And I was so envious of that unacknowledged intimacy, the knowledgeable bickering that they knew each other so well. I wanted to have someone who got on my nerves even. I wanted someone who could do that. And to put out the hand and there's nothing . . . And the other end of that is when you do have that, it's sexy.

The other end of it is, you know, when you're not reading in bed and she's gone to sleep, or you can sit and you roll over and you suddenly hug, cuddle each other, and then you're at it, or just seriously fuck-off horny. Or she is, and you are, like, 'Get off!' It doesn't happen as often, and I'm glad about that, really. If you're in a rock 'n' roll band, literally, you've shagged the world, you know? I mean, it's not even a question of believing your luck. You get so used to it and, I don't know about the other guys, but sometimes I didn't even want it, I just felt I had to. When you're all so lonely – 'How many months have we been out [on the road] now?' And OK, here's someone to hold on to for the night, and I suppose I've got to shag them, fuck it. But it gets like that, so you'll get there. Don't worry about it.

T: The last thing I wanted to ask you about, I know that you're a big William Butler Yeats fan.

BG: Yep.

T: And off the top of your head, would you have a poem of his?

BG: I'll get it wrong, but if you want me to give it a go. All of those of you who know it by heart, forgive me:

> *Had I the heavens' embroidered cloths,*
> *Enwrought with golden and silver light,*
> *The blue and the dim and the dark cloths*
> *Of night and light and the half-light,*

I would spread the cloths under your feet:
But I, being poor, have only my dreams;
I have spread my dreams under your feet;
Tread softly because you tread on my dreams.

Imagine just writing that. That would do me. 'What did you do in your life?'

'I wrote that poem.'

He wishes for the cloths of heaven. Even the name.* Wow.

* 'Aedh Wishes for the Cloths of Heaven'.

Brendan O'Carroll

*'I was a waiter for fifteen years and I like to think that at the
time I was a funny waiter, part of the entertainment . . .
There's very little difference between an audience of four
and an audience of four thousand.'*

Tommy: Wow, how are you? The last time I saw you, you
went through a phase wearing the glasses at the top of the
head.

Brendan O'Carroll: Yeah, that was when I just needed
them for reading. Now I need them all the time. When I
needed them for reading, I'd have them on top of my head
because I literally couldn't see anything, and then they just
got worse, as they do when you get older, Tommy.

T: Tell us, what's America like?

BOC: At the moment, it's bonkers. It's hard to believe, it's
much more provincial than Ireland is. We live in a place
called Davenport, and our local newspaper is the *Davenport
Village*. If it doesn't happen in Davenport, it's not in the
Davenport Village. It could happen in New York, it could
happen anywhere or anything big – they're very, very local.
Especially where we are in Florida, they think Trump is
God. It's weird, it's weird.

T: When you move to a place like that you have to have
two connections.

BOC: OK . . .

T: One is with the place and the second is with the people. So even though you can say these people are very localized, what's your grá for them, like?

BOC: Well, for me, it's not just the American people, it's just foreign people. I'm the youngest in a family of eleven, and most of them emigrated. So when I was nine years of age I went to a private school 'recommended by a judge'. After graduating from there, my mother decided it'd be a good idea to keep me out of trouble during the summers when we were off school to keep sending me to different sisters or brothers around the world. So I got to visit lots of different places, like California, Toronto, a lot of times in London, so I got used to meeting lots of different people.

T: How long are you over there?

BOC: Eighteen years now. Nineteen this year. What happened was, I had been gigging in New York and came back from New York in early 1994 after gigging there, and Tim O'Connor, who was head of RTÉ Sport, said to me, 'Listen, the [Republic of Ireland football] team are going to be based in Orlando, Florida.' Florida was never on my radar, and he said, 'We'd like you to go out there for RTÉ and do a few pieces during the World Cup; you'll have to stay with the team, travel with the team.' It really was one of those, when he said, 'Let's talk money,' I'm thinking I hope he doesn't want too fucking much for this. I went out and what happened was the gig I had was three minutes to camera every second day, which for you and me would be a piece of you-know-what! I got bored so I started driving around Orlando and getting lost and finding new places, and I fell in love with the place. So as soon as the opportunity arose, it was always my intention. I started going back again. I'm a Disney head – I still believe in Santa Claus and I still believe in fairies and I believe in Disney. So every time I landed in Orlando, I felt like I was five years of age. Can't wait to get to Disney, can't wait to get to the magic kingdom. So Jenny and I were going there two or three times a year and giving all of our money to Mickey – which is probably proper mickey money – and then we just decided, you know, I got a nice book deal from Penguin, in 1998 I think it was. I said, 'Rather than do anything else with it, let's buy a house, let's settle down.'

T: And you're fine with the weather over there, are you? With the heat and everything?

BOC: I love it, are you kidding me? For Jaysus' sake, I grew up in a fuckin' fridge! That amazes me, because when we're out doing signings after the UK show, like, you'd be in Glasgow, snow would be falling, icicles hanging out of your nose, and you're signing autographs outside, and somebody will say, 'I believe you live in Orlando,' and I go, 'Yes.' 'Why?' And I go, 'It's a really nice place to live!' But yeah, I do, I like the heat. I couldn't afford the lifestyle that I have there here. Does that make sense?

T: No . . .

BOC: OK, well, the first house we ever bought was a four-bedroom house with a pool in a secure community – it was $160,000 for the house. That here, I couldn't afford it. So the lifestyle is a lot cheaper. Stupid things like, you eat a lot less, and it's not just like this in January. I get up in the mornings here when I lived in Hollystown and I look out the back at twelve o'clock in the day and the automatic lights have come on and you realize this is as bright as it's going to get today. Whereas, in Florida, you wake up to a sparkling blue sky every day, and I swear to God, it really does change your mood. I used to think that Seasonal Affective Disorder,

SAD, was a made-up thing, but it really does make a difference. It does give you a lift.

T: How's your health in general?

BOC: Much better now, much better than I thought it
was. I didn't know I was sick.

T: I didn't know you were sick?

BOC: No, what happened was there's a wonderful doctor
called Alan Byrne, who's the head of the FAI's [Football
Association of Ireland] medical panel. So he asked myself
and Jenny to come down to the FAI for a meeting and, basically, what he wanted to do was, there's a thing called Sudden
Adult Death [Sudden Arrhythmic Death Syndrome], and it
affects kids, really young kids who are dropping dead on a
football pitch out of nowhere, so it's something you always
worry about when they're playing sport. So he brought us
down and made a pitch to us: 'Look, we'd like you to put
sixty thousand quid into this and with that sixty thousand
quid we'll be able to test the U14, U15, U16 . . . all the young
kids on the international teams right up as far as the U21s.'

We listened to this man and his passion – I love passion, I
love a hustler – so I said to him, 'Well, what's your dream?'
and he said, 'Well, obviously, to test every kid. But there's ten
thousand of them, and it would take three years and you're
looking at half a million.' Jenny and I said, 'Well, do it, we'll
fund it. Do it, test every kid, because we have six grandsons,
all of which play sport.'

Ironically, sadly, two weeks before that, a friend of a friend
of ours, their kid was playing football in Skerries and he col-
lapsed on the pitch, but where the pitch was they couldn't get
the ambulance in, so it took them ten minutes to get stuff
over the gate and into the kid and he didn't make it. That
first ten minutes is crucial, so part of what we're doing is

teaching kids and club members how to use a defibrillator, supplying clubs with defibrillators, teaching referees how to do CPR and how to use defibrillators, so if every coach and every referee knows how to use a defibrillator there'll be three people who know how to resuscitate a child. So we put our funds into that.

I've been waiting to get stuff done on my leg, I have CAP, CAD, or whatever the fuck it is, something – I've *something* wrong with my legs! I was trying to get an appointment to get it done here, but every time I was here they could only give me an appointment when I was in America or Australia or whatever, and then same when I was away. When we were going down to the launch of the FAI thing, Jenny said to me, 'Why don't you say it to Dr Byrne, can he pull a few strings and maybe get you seen to?' I hate jumping queues, it really bothers me. She said, 'I know you do, but we've got to get it done.' So I said it to him.

T: And you've given half a million!

BOC: Well, apart from that! He said, 'Leave that with me, I'm actually glad you said it to me, I'll get you seen to.' So he sent me to the Beacon, and a surgeon came out, great guy, looked about twelve. And I told him the story, so he said, 'I'm going to do this test, that test, that scan, this scan' – went through a whole list of stuff. 'Look,' I said, 'if you give me a schedule for that, I'll make sure I'm here in Ireland for all of those.' 'No, no,' he said, 'we'll do them today.' Did all that – at one stage put me out for one of the tests, and when I came to, Jenny said to me, 'He just put a stent in your heart.' I said, 'Really?' He said, 'I found one of your arteries was 95 per cent blocked. You were about a month away from a heart attack.' He said the heart attack wouldn't have killed me but I would have had a weak heart from then on. He said, 'You're 100 per cent.'

I said, 'What about my leg?' and he said, 'I don't do legs.' He said Dr Byrne had rang him and said to him he'd seen me on *The Late Late Show* and I was gasping for breath! Ironically, the day we launched [the defibrillator fund], one of the reporters said, 'You know, Brendan, half a million euro is an awful lot of money to be putting into something,' and I said, 'Yes, it is, but if it saves one life, is it not worth it?' Mine! It's amazing that way, karma.

T: In a general way, would you have looked after yourself over the years?

BOC: I'm not a gym guy. I don't drink. I'm not a gambler.

T: Did you ever drink?

BOC: I'd have the odd one – vodka, because I can't taste it, you know? Vodka and coke, but I wouldn't be a drinker, no.

T: Smoking, or anything like that?

BOC: Oh god, yeah, I love my smoke. I know it's going to kill me, but, you know . . .

T: You still puff away?

BOC: Yeah. I'd look stupid doing nothing. Like they say, if you stop smoking, you'll live another ten years, but I don't think you do, I think it just feels like ten years.

T: Do you have a sense of having made it in terms of your work and your career and that?

BOC: Interesting question, I've never . . .

T: Just to frame it in my imagination and yours, coming from someone else – you can't get bigger than *Mrs Brown*. I mean, I remember touring Australia, and I'd be playing a thousand-seater, and then hearing you're playing a fifteen-to-twenty-thousand-seater. It's been a phenomenal success. I know, with ego, when success happens, a part of you is thinking, yeah, why not? But I'm just wondering, in your sense of self, is there a feeling of accomplishment?

BOC: Well, yeah, there's a feeling of accomplishment every time you walk off the stage, and that you've completed a night. There's always a great sense of accomplishment there because you're terrified going on every night, you know – 'This is the night they're going to find out I'm only a waiter.' And then you come off thinking, oh, they didn't find out, woo! The words 'made it' – I think you have to define what the words 'made it' mean.

T: For yourself.

BOC: No, I understand that. But 'made it' would mean that you had a target or you had a goal to be in a particular place and you get there, so I've 'made it'. I never had a goal, honest to God, Tommy, I never had a goal. My mother had a great saying about success. She said, 'Sometimes success is like disco music. Don't analyse it, just dance to it.' That's what I've been doing, I've just been dancing to it, dancing to it, dancing to it. As it's going on, of course, when you walk into an arena with fifteen thousand people there, you know, there's two feelings: 'Wow!' and the other is 'What the fuck are they expecting?' But then, there's no difference, and I learned that. I mean, I was a waiter for fifteen years and I like to think that at the time I was a funny waiter, part of the entertainment when they wanted it at a table. There's very little difference between an audience of four and an audience of four thousand. You still have to have your timings right, know what you're going to do. Or if you don't know what you're going to do, be like you or I – like you and I would be two of the best off the cuff, I'd say.

T: Yes. We. Would. Brendan . . . !

BOC: Yeah, go ahead, I'm listening! So, you have to define 'am I happy?' Absolutely. Have I got more than I ever

66

dreamed I would ever have? Absolutely. So is that the thing that brings me joy? No, it's not. The thing that brings me joy is I walk out onstage every night dressed as a woman and the girl that comes on to play my daughter is my wife. That gets weird, but it's funny. Buster Brady is my son; Maria is my daughter; Bono, who plays Mrs Brown's grandson, is really my grandson; Trevor, who plays Mrs Brown's son, is my son-in-law. When we go to Australia for six weeks, we go en masse as a family. Nothing gives me more joy than being with my grandkids. Every morning when we're on tour they knock at the door for a cup of tea at eight in the morning.

T: Can you talk to me about happiness and what that feels like, and what is the nature of happiness?

BOC: Not enough people ask that question. A lot of people confuse being *not unhappy* with being happy. Being *not unhappy* is not happy. Being *not unhappy* just means you're not unhappy and you're prepared to settle for that. Nobody has to settle for anything. Every single one of us is entitled to be happy. And sometimes, to make the changes in your life to have that happiness, there are choices, difficult choices. It could be leaving a job, a job that you've been in that pays well but you're dreadfully unhappy in it, or you're *not unhappy*, but you're not happy in it. To take the risk and try something. Happiness is trying. Happiness is not the end, it's the journey. Happiness is finding more out about you.

Even the stage I'm at, I'm still trying to find out what I can't do. To keep putting stuff to BBC and RTÉ and have them turn it down and go, 'Well, I know I can't do that because they looked at it and said, "No, that's shit."' Unfortunately, when you get old enough and you haven't realized that, by the time you get to that stage you realize, ah man, I'm here now but I missed the journey. My absolute nightmare was someday having a million pounds in the bank but not being able to get out of the bed to spend it. To be eighty-five and think, I made it, hahaha, I think I just shit myself again. That's not happiness. Happiness is enjoying the journey and making the journey as comfortable for everyone around you as you can. I don't know if that's answered your question, but that's it.

T: I suppose it's a bit more active than I thought . . .

BOC: Did you think that happiness was a still state?

T: Yeah, maybe.

BOC: Well, do you remember moments in your life when you were happy?

T: Yeah, like, in my life now, I wouldn't describe myself as a happy person.

BOC: But that's your fault.

T: Yeah, eh . . .

BOC: No, really, and I'm not accusing you when I say that.

T: Well, talk to me about that then, about what you mean by that.

BOC: There's a thing you do with PMA, when practising a positive mental attitude; when you get out of bed in the morning and you don't feel happy or you don't feel great, go to the mirror and say, 'I feel fantastic. Oh, I feel fantastic.' And for the next hour, pretend you're happy, pretend you're fantastic, and by the end of that hour you will be happy and you will be fantastic. You'll be happy to do whatever it is, whether that's going to a play with your kids or going to court – it doesn't matter. You're going to be happy, you're going to feel a state of happiness. That state of happiness is active, it's in action. Most things are in action, you know.

I have a weird thing, and I don't want to blow your mind

with it, but I adored my mother, simply adored her. My dad died when I was only nine, so I grew up with my mother, it was me and her, because I was the youngest of the kids. She was a very sharp woman and she would see things coming down the line, so I'd be trying something and she would know that this is not going to work. And she would say to me, 'Bring this to a close, bring it to a close now.' She always finished things: 'Bring this to a close now because it's not going to work so move on to the next thing.' So I never failed – I never had a failure. Everything was going grand. The best thing she ever did for me, as it turns out, is die. She died when I was twenty-eight, and for the next five years every single thing I touched just went to crap. I thought, I'm a complete loser. But I started to realize that you learn nothing by succeeding, it's only in failing when you find yourself. How you cope with things is where you find your strength. The happiness thing – and I'm not talking to you in particular – it's not going to find you, you have to find it. You can't sit at home and go, 'Where's my happiness?' Go find it.

The weird thing I'm talking about is I did a movie called *Sparrow's Trap*, and it absolutely crucified me. I spent more money than I had and I owed more money than I ever could owe. Very, very dark days, and there were two days that I remember really well where I didn't even open the curtains, I didn't get dressed, I didn't turn on the lights. Got up in the morning, made tea and sat in the dark and went back to bed. That second morning, before I went back to bed, I did something that I hadn't done for many years, and I'm not even sure if I've done it since. Just before I went to bed I got on my knees beside my bed like a kid and I joined my hands. My mother used to say, 'Figure it out yourself.' I said, 'Mam, I know you said, "Figure it out yourself," and I know you

was important for me that they'd all understand everything that all these people do around you to make you look good.

T: What's been the most surprising thing about success?

BOC: Funny, my mam warned me about this. She said, 'You're going to struggle and struggle and struggle for success in some form, but as soon as you achieve it, the first thing that's going to strike you is *that was so easy*.' I think what she was trying to tell me was, I tried to be so many things, I tried to be a publisher, tried to be this and that. I needed to be me. The time that I am most myself, particularly in stand-up, when I get on that stage, it's me and the microphone and nowhere to hide, so I just bare my balls. You know, you do it, so you know what I'm talking about. It is terrifying, but I am the most myself when I'm doing that. That's me in the raw. When you come offstage and think, I had two hours of being me and I loved it. That's . . .

T: When you say being *you*, though . . .

BOC: I spent my life saying the things I thought people wanted to hear. I was a worker to supervisors who couldn't think half as quick as I could, but I would tell them they were wonderful because they kept me in my job. I did what I thought was the right thing because I didn't want people to think ill of me or whatever, and it's not about that. It's recognizing that you look in the mirror and say, 'I'm a good guy, I'm a really nice guy, and I do my best to do the right thing. I don't always succeed, because I'm human, but I know I'm doing my best. I fucking like you.' And I do. I like me. So when you like you, you start to be you more. The problem is, you're afraid if somebody finds out that you do particular things in your life, or whatever, that they will think less of you. Who cares what anybody thinks of you, honest to God? What you think of yourself, that's all that matters.

T: You're quite remarkable.

BOC: That's very kind of you, thank you.

T: You have . . . I don't know if self-belief is the right word, but you're . . .

BOC: Cocky!

T: No, no, it's not that. I don't know what it is. Maybe it's an energy or a commitment.

BOC: I'm hopeful that if you blank your mind, and it's one of the things I did before I came out, and before I did the very first *Late Late Show* I ever did. I spent the weeks before it going, 'If he says this, I'll say that. If he asks that question, I'll do this.' Then I went, 'What are you doing?' You're doing it again, you're trying to be somebody else. I don't know what you're going to ask. It's immaterial what you're going to ask, but you didn't want to talk to Mrs Brown, you didn't want to talk to somebody who is pretending, you wanted to talk to me. So I blanked everything out and said, 'I'll answer the questions as me,' in the hope that, you know, you, that whatever dilemma comes at you, or whatever question comes at you, whatever situation comes at you, the thing that will come to the fore with you because, you know, you're being yourself, is the right thing. Or certainly the right thing as you know it. Because, at the end of the day, everybody wants to do the right thing.

There's a belief out there that people in general are malicious, particularly Irish people, when it comes to success. 'Oh, look at him in his Jag' – I don't have a Jag, by the way, I have a Skoda. But the thing is, people aren't malicious. Again, I come back to my mother. She said to me, 'Brendan, you have to understand that everybody is having a tough day.'

T: Can I ask ya a queer one now. It just came into my head there. So you carry your mother. She might be dead, but she's still alive in you . . .

BOC: Oh, Jesus, yeah.

T: And you dress up as a woman.

BOC: Wow, I don't know, there could be problems there!

T: Do you look like her when you have the stuff on?

BOC: No. Well, a little bit, probably. She was a big woman, a very big woman. No, people used to say to me when they read the book and I was doing a book tour in America, they'd ask, 'Is Mrs Brown based on your mom?' And I'd say, 'No, no, she's not because my mum was just extraordinary. She began her life as a nun, she had eleven kids, so she was obviously right not to be a nun . . .'

T: Didn't go back to the convent after the eleventh kid! *'It was all a big mistake!'*

BOC: No, she misread her vocation altogether! She went on to teach languages and then was fired because she married my dad and a married woman couldn't teach then. Then she went to the union and all that, and eventually became the first Irish woman to be elected to the Irish parliament as a Labour TD, while she had eleven kids and we lived in a two-room house with an outdoor toilet. She was just quite an extraordinary woman. So no, not Mrs Brown, but actually, I think Mrs Brown is like my mum, except she doesn't have the education. She doesn't have that degree from Galway University that my mother had. She has a wisdom, though, that my mother had. That wisdom is based around: *it has to be good for the family.*

I often say that men and women make decisions in very different ways. A man, and including myself in this, the first thing that will strike you when you're making a decision about something that's offered to you is, 'I don't know, will this be good for me?' A woman given the same decision will go, 'I don't know how this will affect the family.' They seem to think in a different way. Now, that may sound sexist, but that's just been my experience. I think Agnes is like that. To Agnes Brown, it's about the family. Sure, if you killed someone in O'Connell Street, if you shoot them, she'll bate you around the house. Then she'd get the shovel and help you bury the body. Because you're her clan and she is that mother hen that wants to keep them all safe, and we all do, as parents, we want to keep our kids safe. That's why when they do things that you're so disappointed in, it guts you.

Family is very, very important to me. To have somebody in your life – I have Jenny, thank God. The rest of the world doesn't give a shit about you, Tommy, trust me. Maybe for the time that you're on TV they like you, but after that they don't think about you. They don't think about me, but I've got someone in my life who every single day cares how I am. And that's so fucking rare. If you can find that, snap it up, baby . . . I don't care about her!

T: Do you have wounds?

BOC: This is going to sound now like I'm spoofing you, but I'm not a revenge person. Honestly, I don't ever go, 'I'll have him.' I couldn't care less . . .

T: No, not necessarily wounds that someone has hurt you, but scars.

BOC: Emotional scars? Fuck, yeah. There's things that you don't surmount. My mother passing away, that was really tough. Having said that, I didn't cry, because I was organizing everything, as she lived with me for the rest of her life until she died. So I was organizing the funeral, organizing flying the family home from wherever they were, and getting everything ready, and I did all that. I didn't cry because there was nothing left unsaid. My mother had no doubt that I loved her. No doubt whatsoever, and I had no doubt that she absolutely loved me. There was nothing left to be said, it wasn't like, 'If only I got a chance to say this.' I did, I got it, I said it. But I moved on, and twenty years it took me. I was sitting in New York in the Fitzpatrick Hotel and I had just been asked to read in this place in New York I knew about because my mother had talked to me about it when I was younger. I sat there and I thought, I'm about to read there, she'd love that, and I just fell apart. So much so that when Jenny came and joined me I couldn't even tell her what was wrong with me. So, yeah, that was a wound.

I was very young when my son died. That was a wound, because he was a first child and, like everybody else, I had all the things figured out in my head – white picket fence, swing in the garden, he'd play football, just like his dad did, I'd go to the games with him, blah blah blah. It changed overnight, and it leaves a hole. I'm very lucky to have three fantastic kids, but they don't fill that gap. Not that you want them to, but they don't. But other than that, Tommy, I'm fine!

T: I wasn't aware of that, Brendan, that you had a son that died.

BOC: Yeah, Brendan Junior.

T: When was that?

BOC: Nineteen seventy-nine. He would have been twenty-one at the turn of the millennium.

T: How old was he when he died?

BOC: Just a couple of weeks. But then Fiona came along, then Danny came along, then Eric came along. I lived up to what I wanted to be. I wanted to be a father, and I was.

T: You're wild craic onstage, Brendan. There's a wildness to *Mrs Brown*. I think the show came into criticism from people in the industry who maybe just couldn't understand its popularity, couldn't understand the common touch that you had. Every time I watch it, it makes me laugh. As a fellow professional, I can see some of the jokes coming down the line, but it makes absolutely no difference because the spirit . . .

BOC: But the thing is, the audience see the jokes. The audience know what's going to come on the punchline, and if we don't deliver that punchline, they'll be so disappointed. They know it's coming, but they're waiting for the punchline and for Agnes to say it.

T: But you do it with such joy and abandon, Brendan, and I think that's the attractive thing about it.

BOC: Oh, well, thank you. I love it. I love her.

Brian D'Arcy

*'One of the things that celibacy does is you
become so concerned about not falling in celibacy
that celibacy becomes more important than your
priesthood. I think that's awful.'*

Tommy: Wasn't that a coincidence – me talking about the
Pope and everything! You probably teleported in from some
other place.

Brian D'Arcy: I'm on my way to Medjugorje!

T: Is that how you pronounce it?

BD: It's how I pronounce it anyway . . .

T: Where in the north are you from?

BD: I'm from County Fermanagh and I've lived in Mount
Argus in Dublin for most of my life.

T: Is that like a prison?

BD: Very. Because we actually called our rooms cells. To
us, it was like a prison.

T: What is Mount Argus?

BD: It's a monastery and parish. One of the most famous
churches in Dublin for years and years. The guys in the 1916
Rising went to confession there before they went down. I
was there for nearly twenty years, then I went to Enniskillen,
where I'm from, to a monastery there called the Graan, a
great place too. About a year and a half ago they decided, at
seventy-three years of age, to shift me to County Down, so

I'm in there in Crossgar, where Ian Paisley founded his first church. I think there's a message for me in that somewhere, but I haven't found it yet.

T: God, you'd be doing well to get a message out of that! Talk to me about 'the ride'.

BD: Excuse me?

T: Talk to me about the ride, about sex, and about your own experiences. Your feeling of sexuality. Not personally speaking, but also culturally-speaking and how we are.

BD: Yeah . . . well, it's going to be a short show – I know very little about it!

T: It might have crossed your mind once or twice, like!

BD: Yeah, it did. Well, I suppose I'm kind of famous for saying – or not famous for saying but I've been consistent in saying – really since I was ordained, that the idea of the priests having to be celibate was absolute nonsense. And I still think that. So it's an extremely good question because, basically, I think the thing that is most wrong with the Catholic Church, and indeed Christian churches in general, is that the development of people as human beings has gone far ahead of the theology of the Catholic Church. And our theology of sexuality is just gone – we're miles behind it. I think all the Christian churches are, but the Catholic Church is the one I know best.

It's about thirty years since I married a couple who did not live at the same address. And yet we're saying that they shouldn't live together before they're married. People find each other, and they're trying to find out if they're suited to each other. Whether I like it or not, that's what people are doing, and they're happy with it. And why should I be telling them it's a sin – and I'm not sure it is – if they're in love and happy and progressing and finding out [about each other].

Relationships are not just about lust, and it's a lot more than that. Our theology says relationships are about lust and lust is forbidden, and that's why nobody passes much remarks about [the Church] now – because what we're saying is irrelevant.

T: Was it ever a make-or-break thing for you in terms of your own sexual desires and so forth?

BD: It was, Tommy, it was. I think probably most people know this. I was lucky enough to fall in love one time, and I had to make a choice. Obviously, if you're in love with somebody, you don't make a choice on your own. It has to be a joint choice. And it was make-or-break at that time. And I think it was more that the person didn't want to take me away from the priesthood. I felt extremely angry with myself and with everybody else that I had to make a choice between love and priesthood. And I still feel angry about that, because I don't think it's a fair choice and I don't think it's a necessary choice. But the bottom line of it is that you have to content yourself, and I really do want to be a priest.

T: How old were you when that happened?

BD: Probably in my mid-thirties. It was over a period of time. And it was at a stage where I had been over ten years a priest. The first year I was a priest, I thought I knew everything. I had the answer to every question that nobody was asking. By three or four years I was a different person. And then I started writing for the *Sunday World* around that time and the whole thing just developed completely after that because people kept writing to me, hundreds and hundreds and hundreds of letters a week. And they thought I was a human being, and I didn't feel like a human being. I had been abused as a young fella and had been abused as a student on the way to the priesthood. So all of that came as a huge thing and took me a long time to sort myself out. And I'm not sure that I've sorted myself out yet, actually. In fact, most days I'd say to myself, 'I hope you haven't,' because life's a journey, and when you think you have it sorted out, you have stopped living and you're half dead. You have to keep going.

T: The people that abused you, what happened to them?

BD: They died without anybody knowing it. I was ten when a brother abused me at school, and I was eighteen, going on nineteen, when I was abused in the monastery. And so it has taken me a long time to do it. At the moment I'm just trying to write a little bit about that within myself, because I feel that if you don't write about it or talk about it or think about it or externalize it some way, no matter what age you are . . . the older I am getting now – is really what I'm trying to say – the older I'm getting the more the effects of the abuse are destroying me.

T: How?

BD: Because you feel that your life has been wasted. That I've done nothing. I've worked as hard as I could, work eighteen hours a day and still do, doing mostly what a priest would do, trying to mix with people, trying to learn with people, trying to be at pop concerts and Masses and bedsides and crematoriums and jails . . . you learn from each of them and you try to be 'compassion', because I think that's the big word. There's a bit of this in Matthew's Gospel, where they used to translate it as being 'perfect as your Heavenly Father is perfect', and Scripture scholars discovered that that was a mistranslation. It is 'your Heavenly Father is compassionate'.

I belong to an order called the Passionists, so if I have not been compassionate, then I'm not much of a priest and I'm certainly not much of a Passionist either. But it is increasingly difficult, Tommy, to be as compassionate as I want to be in a society that has lost the will to be compassionate, in a society where sin is tolerated but never forgiven. Failure in society at the moment is really the ultimate vulnerability in life. And that's going to kill us because you simply cannot live in a life without failure and without mistakes and without forgiveness for those mistakes.

When I say forgiveness, I'm not talking about confession, though I do believe in confession. What I'm really talking about is if I can't look in the mirror and say that you've made mistakes, you're not perfect, you're never going to be God, no matter what you think you are. If I can't forgive myself for those things, how can I hand on anything to somebody else unless I've dealt with myself? One of the things that celibacy does is you become so concerned about not falling in celibacy that celibacy becomes more important than your priesthood. I think that's awful.

T: I had an instance once when I was about nineteen, where I was working in a hostel for homeless men and I went upstairs with one of them. There was a degree of innocence with me, you know. He started to rub my leg and then brought his hand up to my groin and started to unzip my fly, and I got myself out of the situation. But when I think back on it, I wonder why I allowed him to go from my thigh into my groin.

BD: Yes, at ten, I didn't know what was happening. I mean, I didn't even know it was abuse until years afterwards. That may sound stupid, but that's the way it is. At eighteen, I was nervous, I was young, I'd been destroyed by the earlier abuse. And you want to be a people-pleaser, and you want to always do something that will ingratiate yourself, that you don't want to be rejected because you've already been rejected.

T: When you say 'destroyed by the earlier abuse', what do you mean?

BD: I stopped being a child at ten. Two things happen – you either become extremely angry and try to act as an adult, or you freeze emotionally.

T: Can I ask you what was the nature of the abuse when you were ten?

BD: Yeah, well, that's never a good question to ask in a public place, but I know you're honest in asking it. So I will give you a rough description of it. At ten, I was from a country area in County Fermanagh, and at that stage in the north of Ireland, unless you passed the Eleven-plus examination, Catholics couldn't get an education. But if you passed the Eleven-plus, you got a free education. The little school that I was at had nobody who ever passed the exam. So my aunt was in Omagh, and my father and my mother and her agreed that I seemed a cheeky little boy and if they brought me to Omagh, that her son, who was my cousin, was the teacher and I would pass the Eleven-plus, which is what I did. So at ten years of age I went down to Omagh, which is thirty-something miles from Enniskillen, every Sunday night, and lived with my aunt and washed dishes and so forth to pay for my keep. And so on Friday night I was just mad to get home, back to Enniskillen, which I did by train at that stage. And I was a lonely country kid in a townie school. Are you country or townie?

T: A bit of both, really.

BD: So you know what it means. A country kid has his own cuteness, but he's not cute enough for townies at that age. So I'd have been in the schoolyard and probably standing a little bit away out from it, not playing football or whatnot, because that was the nature of it. And the brother spotted me, and during lunchtime he'd bring me up to his room, and he'd say now . . . he'd be very nice to me, and 'I want to do this to you,' and he gave me sweets, and 'You're very lonely-looking.' And then he just put me across his knee and abused me enough so that he could get satisfaction. I was a vulnerable kid. It was that grooming thing.

T: You mentioned about being eighteen and feeling that your life had been destroyed. When did that penny drop of what had happened to you?

BD: Probably during secondary school during the five years of St Michael's College, which I went back to after I passed the Eleven-plus. It was probably during that year. You're growing up. Hormones change. You're playing football and all the rest of it, and you hear guys talking about some guys to keep away from. And I began to get ferociously guilty, as in, was I involved in this? Had I committed a sin? I was afraid to say it. You didn't tell – who was going to believe a ten-year-old country kid? I used to get scared at night and I could feel ferociously dirty. And so I never really had a healthy attitude towards sex or sexuality at all.

I had never thought of being a priest because I was a reasonable footballer and that's all I was interested in, but I went to confession, as we normally did in those days, and the priest said to me, 'You should think about becoming a priest.' And, you see, instantly, I did, because I was afraid to say no, but my mother and father didn't want me to be a priest. What happened was, eventually, I thought that I had to give it a try. That's just the nature of me. We went to Knock, and I didn't know that Our Lady didn't appear there [*BD laughs*], that she was on her way to Medjugorje! But anyway, I prayed there, so she heard me. And on the way back, my mother said, 'Do you still want to?' I said I wanted to try, and so at seventeen

I entered on the first of September 1962, which is a long time ago. And I'm still there, even though at times the Vatican didn't want me to be there. Others didn't want me to be there.

By the time I came to Mount Argus as a student and the man just took advantage of me because, again, he could see that I was a helpful, compassionate young guy. And thin for my age, and immature because of what had happened to me before, though I was wiser at that time. But like yourself, you say, 'In the name of Jeepers, how did I get myself caught again?' Why? Because the survivor always blames themselves. But I got through it, and I found my voice after I was ordained through music, bands and friends, going to dances every night. I got it from the university of the world.

T: Can I ask you about this notion, though, of the wounded healer and that sometimes it's only those who have suffered hugely and have been hurt who are capable of healing others? That the fact that those things have happened to you, in some curious way it gives you a vulnerability that allows you to heal other people.

BD: I'm with you up until that last sentence. I'm not sure that I am a healer. I'm not sure of that. I'm not sure, that is, that I should even attempt to be a healer. I see healing as something from within rather than from without. But I think what it did give me, Tommy, was the courage to speak truth to power. And you know, the famous night in this studio with the Cardinal* and things like that, I'm sure if I hadn't had to survive abuse, I wouldn't have had the same conviction when I was speaking. Any institution that puts

* Father D'Arcy confronted Cardinal Cahal Daly live on *The Late Late Show* in November 1995 about the Church's attitude to clerical sexual abuse scandals.

the good name of that institution ahead of the vulnerability of a child deserves no respect.

T: Your life now, what does it involve?

BD: It involves a lot of things, writing for the *Sunday World* . . . That is a great thing because I learned a huge thing and that is that I had almost a parish of my own in the *Sunday World*, where people wrote to me and I wrote to them about things. I got a freedom from it, and it was a great paper to be in because no bishop ever read it! And so I was on my own there, saying what I wanted to say, and people appreciated that. For twelve years, I went to the dancehalls of Dublin every night. The showband lads were old friends of mine and I went and stood there, and all kinds of people would come up every night to talk to me, to ask me something or tell me something. Why? Because I was there, and that was it. I learned from them, and I think they might have learned something from me. I think what they learned from me was that the world wasn't bad. You could go to a dance, you could go out with a girl, you could be with a girl, you could enjoy yourself. And feck it, there's nothing wrong with it. The clergy had an image of being spoilsports, putting a stick between people in case they got too close at dances and so forth.

T: So did guards at one stage. No, seriously. I was courting in the doorway of a credit union one time and a guard shined a light and told both of us to clear off and get home. So it wasn't just priests.

BD: Yeah, all I want to know is, Tommy, did you get the loan?!

T: Well, whatever I gave her, she gave me something different back, with interest!

BD: I'm fifty years a priest now this year. I'm at the end of my days. I don't need to say I've done anything good. I leave it to a higher authority than me. God is love. He sees what I've done, he'd know that I made mistakes. He'd know that I was a failure in many ways. He'd also know that so was Jesus on the cross a failure. You mentioned a bit earlier about the wounded healer. And that's what it is. The vulnerability of failure. I always love the idea that, on the cross, Jesus had his hands and feet nailed to a piece of wood, he could move neither hand nor foot. And that's when salvation happened. Out of failure comes new life.

T: That's a very countercultural message.

BD: Yes, and I have no problem with that. I agree. But I have enough experience in life to know that unless you recognize that, you'll end up against a blank wall. We do need something to look forward to. We do need a bigger picture. We do need a perspective on our wee journey. Our journey is beautiful and brilliant and perfect, but there needs to be a perspective in it. It's not just my journey – it's my journey with *our* journey. And there has to be a difference. The day we forget about others, or especially the vulnerable, the young and the old and the sick and the prisoners and the people who hadn't had a chance in life, unless we can somehow take care of them . . . I'm not talking about religion. I'm talking about a society that hasn't got the values that takes care of those who are least able to take care of themselves, then that society is nothing but a selfish society that will self-destruct sooner rather than later.

T: But it's not only a societal thing, it's an individual thing.

BD: Yes. I am saying that.

T: It's up to you and me and everybody to take care of, or to allow, or not suppress that part of us which is defeated and shameful and broken.

BD: And that's absolutely right. Exactly that's what I'm saying. I can handle my failures because I know that through the brokenness I can be pieced together better than when I started out.

Catriona Crowe

*'Fake news is a very dangerous thing because what it means
is opinion supplants fact. The most important question
any informed human being can ask another human being is:
"How do you know what you know?"'*

Tommy: I don't think that I know you.

Catriona Crowe: Yeah, I have you at a huge disadvantage
now, as I know all about you and you know nothing about
me. I could interview you.

T: Eh, it wouldn't be as interesting as you might think.
What's your story?

CC: OK. I am an archivist. I've looked after historical
documents in the National Archives of Ireland for forty
years. I had the privilege of putting the 1901 and 1911 cen-
suses online, free to access for everyone here and abroad to
look at and discover their ancestors, good, bad and indifferent, whenever they wanted to. I also discovered, in 1996, two
thousand files relating to the adoption of Irish children in
America from the 1940s on, which became part of the conversation about that whole distressing, dreadful time when
women were deprived of their children in mother-and-baby
homes and they were shipped off to America for adoption.
That conversation is still going on today, as you know. I've
also spent forty years involved in community development
and politics in the North inner city where I live. I was one of

Tony Gregory's canvassers – the late Tony Gregory – for a very long time. And I have numerous other interests, but we will stick to those ones for the moment.

T: Just to clear something up before we horse into it. You said people's ancestry – you haven't looked at mine, by any chance, have you?

CC: Alas, sir, no, I didn't know enough about you to check it out, but if you give me all the details, sure I'll do it tomorrow.

T: It's funny, I come from one of those families where one side of the family, everyone is available and we know what people did . . .

CC: They're not the Tiernans that all had TB and are identified as the source of the infection?

T: Our reputation precedes us! I'd come from a long line of Mayo Guinness-drinkers . . .

CC: A proud ancestor.

T: Yeah, but the other side of my family is just [all over the place] – and I don't know if this is a common thing, but you're coming across people who were half-related to people, people coming from orphanages, people who were raised by other people, and you'd want the energy and the commitment to find out, it seems. I think it's a very Irish thing. There was a lot of secrets.

CC: There were, and sometimes still are. Like, part of the mission was to be able to put as much information online as possible. So there's a lot more stuff there now than there was twenty years ago. So maybe you searched quite a while ago. If you were to do it again now, you'd have much greater help: their birth certificates and marriage certificates and death certificates, big parish records. Most people in Ireland in the nineteenth century and onwards were Catholic, and those records are now online too and can be searched, so there's probably a good chance if you know a parish, for example, from where that side of your family came that you'd be able to find them.

T: I'd have people on the left-hand side of the family who wouldn't have been using their real name.

CC: How do you distinguish between the left- and the right-hand side of the family?

T: Well, I suppose the right-hand side would be Mayo, on the left-hand side would be dark Tipperary.

CC: I think I understand.

T: Did you do much research into your own family?

CC: I did. I mean, I started work in the Public Record Office, as it was called in the Four Courts in 1974. I declare myself now as one of those 'auld ones' that you're constantly having rants about – you said on one of your programmes that anybody north of sixty is an auld one! Hello!?

T: You should claim it!

CC: Oh, I do, I do. I just want to alert you, sir, to the fact that you'll be there yourself. Not too far away.

T: And let's hope I'm riding auld ones when I get there!

CC: No, I take great pleasure in being an auld one. Anyway, as a young one, when I was a young one, when I started working in that interesting place, which of course had been blown up in 1922 at the beginning of the Civil War, doing away with eight hundred years of Irish history, and the British army didn't do it, the Black and Tans didn't do it, the fairies didn't do it, evil spirits didn't do it. We did it to ourselves. We blew up our own history at the start of our existence as an independent state.

T: But not as a deliberate act?

CC: No, as a by-product of . . . as a historian said to me, 'Stop giving out about this, Catriona. You're always going on about it – when things get going, lads do things.' And I said, 'Can I quote you on that now, sir?', and he said, 'No!' I've got older and wiser and more tolerant. Yes, when things get going, lads *do things*. The fog of war tends to stop people thinking about the unintended consequences of what they're doing. But the fact is that the Anti-Treaty forces were in the Four Courts for three solid months before there was a counter-attack. They were going out to the pub every night, up to Barry's Hotel to have chats with their national army former comrades. Ernie O'Malley and Sean McBride were going up to Grafton Street every day to have coffee with ladies in Robert's Café – *Dublin can be heaven with coffee at eleven* – and three sets of people at least came to them and said, 'Please don't forget that in that building over there is eight hundred years of archives from going back to the twelfth century. Please make sure they're safe.'

T: But what kind of records would have been kept?

CC: Well, the ones that I mourn the most are the census records for Ireland from 1821, '31, '41 and '51, so a complete record of every individual who lived in this country before the Famine. I don't know if you've ever been to the deserted village in Achill. Mayo is your territory. It's a very beautiful, silent place, as you walk along those streets. It's being excavated by archaeologists right now. It is terrible to imagine that we could know the names and occupations and religion and relationships of all of the people who lived in that village in 1841 before the Famine depopulated it. We lost that. They went up in smoke.

There were religious records because, of course, religion was a hugely important part of the administration of the country going back to the twelfth century, court records going back to the thirteenth century. All of those kinds of things – the administrative records, transportation records about people transported to Van Diemen's Land, as many were, prisoner records, everything under the sun. I suppose we're lucky in a way that the man who ran the place, Herbert Wood, wrote the definitive guide to what was there in 1919 so we know everything that perished in 1922, he put it all into a book. He left very soon after the fire, absolutely broken-hearted that everything he had worked so hard to make safe was now gone.

T: What do you think the effect on us would be if we were able to read the names of the people who were deported and that kind of thing?

CC: Anything that adds to our understanding of the complexity of the past is useful. History is a discipline that mercifully has been restored to the curriculum by our most recent Minister for Education, Joe McHugh, and I congratulate him. It was a very, very dangerous decision to remove it. This is a country that needs to understand its history.

T: When you say 'understand our history', what do you mean? What are we lacking?

CC: We're lacking the primary sources for a large portion of it. The big administrative archive for the nineteenth century that was in Dublin Castle in 1922 hadn't been transferred to the Four Courts, so it escaped, so we have that. We have very good prison records, very good court records for the nineteenth and twentieth centuries. It's before that, as we go backwards, that everything becomes sparser. So the seventeenth century in Ireland is the huge period of land transformation. Three quarters of the land of Ireland is moved from Catholic ownership to Protestant ownership.

That is a cataclysmic change and it's the source of a lot of the trouble that came afterwards. We need to understand that fully. We have some records relating to it, but nothing like [what was lost]. I mean, to know what happened, to know who was affected, to know what went on.

People sometimes say history is written down somewhere in a book. When I was working in the archives – I'm now gone for two years, and the great relief is I don't have to get up in the morning any more, which is a marvellous piece of liberation and joy – I would often get letters or phone calls from young people saying, 'Can you send me the bit at the archives about Michael Collins?'

And you'd have to write back and say there is no 'bit' of the archives, there isn't a story written down as a continuous narrative. That's what you read in your history books. But behind that story are documents, and those documents are letters and maps and census returns and legal documents and photographs and all kinds of stuff that give us the complex picture.

T: And what's your understanding of the early 1900s in Ireland?

CC: A very vibrant time of change. We've got the Gaelic Revival going on, which is a huge thing. We've got the GAA going on, and you've got a rediscovery of Ireland as a nation, as a place with an identity of its own. I'm not taking sides on this, by the way. It must have been a fascinating time to be alive.

T: Was there a sense in that of being able to tolerate the English?

CC: Well, the English were tolerated for very long. I mean, half of the British Army was Irish. We've got to remember that, that there were huge connections between Ireland and

England right through the colonial period, and a lot of it wasn't forced. A lot of it was people living their lives.

If most of us think about how we live our lives now, we get on from day to day. What people want is the stuff we're talking about in every election campaign – decent housing, proper health service, jobs, a way to rear your families in peace and quiet, stuff for your children, a decent education system. All of those things are what people generally want and wanted then, so most people got on with it. It's usually a small minority who are anxious to have serious change at the end of the nineteenth century.

T: That doesn't make the change unjustified.

CC: No, not at all. Everything starts with an idea. So when you get an idea of Ireland as a nation that can then aspire to independence, you rapidly get the growth of Sinn Féin, which becomes a party of some significance, but not really until after 1916, when things start to roll ahead.

CC: Our focus needs to move into looking at social history, what happens to particular families in particular places. Hopefully, we'd be able to find your left-hand side of the family along the way and see what interesting stories they have to tell us, but we're focusing a lot more now on social history than we used to, and less on political and military history.

T: When you say 'social history', what do you mean?

CC: I mean the history of ordinary lives, of what kinds of houses people lived in, what clothes they wore, how many children they had, what relationships were like, what marriage was like, when people were born, when they got married, when they died, the costumes that surrounded those things . . .

T: What did people use for contraception?

CC: The withdrawal system, Your Honour.

T: Really? That?

CC: I mean, there's stuff about sheep's bladders and things like that going way, way back. I wouldn't fancy it myself, I have to say. But, generally, there were two methods of contraception: that withdrawal system, and infanticide, and there was a lot of infanticide in Ireland. When women were caught killing their children, up until 1944 it was a capital offence. No woman was hanged for it, but they often spent quite a period of time in jail. In the 1940s, people are starting to understand what postnatal depression is. They're not really thinking about the fact that it can be poverty and fear of family disapproval and the Church that forced women into this situation. But we've come through, thank God, and a lot of that has gone and we're in a much brighter, clearer atmosphere when it comes to how women are treated.

T: Was there a remarkable difference between the city and the country in terms of living standards and opportunity? I read somewhere recently about Gerard Manley Hopkins, the English poet, who was living in Dublin, I think, in the late 1800s . . .

CC: He lived in the top floor of Newman House, which is now the Museum of Irish Literature on Stephen's Green.

T: I was going to say that.

CC: Sorry, I pre-empted you.

T: At that time, he talks about Dublin as being a city of squalor.

CC: The slums in Dublin at the time of the 1911 census – and we know a lot about Dublin in 1911 because the census survives – were probably the worst in Europe. They were worse than London or Birmingham or Glasgow.

T: So would it have been healthier to be out in the country, then?

CC: Much healthier. You were three times more likely as an infant to survive if you lived in the country than if you lived in the city. That doesn't mean there wasn't extreme poverty in the country – there was, but there was clean air and there was decent water, usually from a well nearby.

I know a lot of this first hand because I had the great good fortune when I was a child in the 1950s to be dispatched down the country to my aunt Mary in County Clare to my father's home place for a lot of the summer. I was there at a time when there was a thatched house and there was a well halfway up the road, which I used to collect water. I know exactly what the weight of a bucket of water is when you're carrying it half a mile down the road. She cooked over an open fire. When my lovely cousin from America came to visit and asked where is the toilet, she said, 'There's acres of toilets, take your pick.'

T: There's a massive jacks outside the house!

CC: That's what it is out there. When I'd come, she'd say, 'If you think you're coming down here now to be reading books for the whole summer, you have another think coming to you,' which filled my heart with loathing and horror. But they were wonderful times and I learned what it was like to live as European people had lived for centuries, and as most people in the world still live today, which is something we tend to forget in our extremely comfortable Western life. When I see water coming out of a tap, I still rejoice. If you've carried a bucket of water all the way down from a well halfway up the lane, you don't take that for granted.

T: Do we have an over-romantic view of the past in Ireland?

CC: Possibly and possibly not. Here's an interesting story.

One of the things you asked me about was squalor in Dublin. Dublin was filled with very, very bad tenement houses in 1911. The house in Henrietta Street on the Northside of the city that is now the tenement museum had one hundred people living in it in 1911. One hundred people. Hard for us to imagine now what that was like, you know, kids top to toe in beds, terrible overcrowding, shocking lack of privacy.

When we opened up the census records, there was a TV programme made about it the summer after called *The Tenements*. I was having some work being done on my roof where I live off the North Strand. These lads on the roof fixing it, when I came down that morning, they said, 'You were on the telly last night. You were talking about the tenements. We come from the tenements and we never talk about it.' So I said, 'Let's talk about it now.' So we stood there in my street for half an hour and we talked about their childhoods in the tenements of Dublin.

And it was a mixed story. Some of it was really hard. 'It was really cold in the wintertime and you had to go out and get firewood, and my mam had to work like a dog to keep everything clean and tidy.' And the other half of it was everyone had a wonderful time – 'We were kids, we were out on the street, you could go out and play on the street then, I've made friends I never lost,' you know, all of that close community stuff which is still very much part of the North inner city, where I've had the privilege to live for forty years, and it's to be cherished, that.

So we do [romanticize it], and of course that romantic view of rural Ireland – with no disrespect meant, Alice Taylor has made that into a very rosy vision of life. I had the privilege of seeing you in John B. Keane's *Sive* – I think it was last year – playing that wicked wily little matchmaker

Thomasheen. (You were brilliant, by the way, and you've very nice shins, I'd wanted to say that to you, you were wearing breeches.) John B. Keane was one of the people who first revealed to Ireland – that held up a mirror to its face and said, 'This is what rural Ireland is like; parents are prepared to sell their daughter for money.' That's what *Sive* was about. And he sent that play to the Abbey Theatre, and Ernest Blythe, who was the manager at the time, said, 'There are no people in Ireland like that. We are not showing that play.' John B., who was smart, took it on the amateur circuit. Thousands of people came to see it because they knew what they were seeing was the truth. So everything is a mixture. It's all complicated.

My slogan at all times about history is 'complicate the narrative'. Do not look for black-and-white answers. They're not to be found. Things are far more complicated than we like to think, and when you start doing black-and-white answers, you get what we have in America today, alas. That's what comes out of black-and-white versions of where the world is.

T: It's a hard thing, that notion of approaching the past. I suppose next year is the beginning of the remembrance of the Civil War.

CC: No, the Civil War doesn't start until 1922.

T: Sorry about that . . .

CC: We've one more year of the wonderfully peaceful War of Independence. This year is going to be hard. Next year it's going to be hard, but at least we can say it was the Black and Tans, it was the auxiliaries, who were *shocking* depredators, dreadful people. Then we're going to have to face our own atrocities. That's going to be the hard one. In 1922/23, it was a short civil war but it killed a lot of people and the results of it are with us to this day.

T: So how do we approach that without being poisoned by it?

CC: Well, if you will indulge me, and this again has been something that a lot of people have called for for this decade of centenaries; what we need is more information now . . .

T: Can I stop you there for a second – when you say 'more information', do you mean that because it's a hundred years ago, we're going to be unearthing stuff? *Your great-grandfather shot my* . . .

CC: Yeah, we need to grow up and deal with it. We really do. And we can. The Bureau of Military History, which the state kept locked up in a strong room in the Department of the Taoiseach from the time it was taken and would not open it up, year after year, [we were] banging on the door saying, 'Please open this up, everyone's cool, it's a long time ago, we can do it.' And we did, and there's all kinds of stuff in that about *my great-grandfather shot so-and-so*, and *so-and-so informed on whoever* and so on. Everyone said, 'Grand.'

We can deal with this now. We're mature enough. It's a hundred years ago, for God's sake. If we don't understand the origins of ourselves as an independent state, how can we hope to make anything of it? So let me just tell people about this because they need to know – the Bureau of Military History is online, you can find it no problem, just put it into the Google search box, and there you will find the oral history of the revolution. If you've anybody in your family who was involved, you will find their statement that they made in their own words, and believe me, it's a magical experience to have that.

T: So hang on – people made a statement?

CC: Yes. In the 1940s, Éamon de Valera, who was Taoiseach at the time, realized that a lot of people who were involved in the revolutionary struggle from 1913 effectively up to the end of the War of Independence were dying. So he set up a thing called the Bureau of Military History, a state agency which was staffed by people who had been members of the national army, the Free State army and members of the Anti-Treaty side from the Civil War, so that they would be able to go and talk to their people and get them to make statements. And they did. They gathered 1,770 statements, some of them two hundred pages long, some of them as short as six pages.

Who didn't make a statement? De Valera himself never made a statement to the Bureau of Military History.

T: I'm just blown away by the idea of all these people saying, almost like a truth and reconciliation committee, 'This is what I saw, this is what I did.'

CC: Yeah, and they did, and because it's in their own words, Tommy, it's incredibly moving. I've seen people break down and cry when they read something from their grandfather who they might never have met or, if they did, that they recognize the voice and the cadences after hearing. It's beautiful.

The other big archive is the pensions records. What matters in this country more than anything else? Pensions, as we know, right? They set up schemes in 1924 when Cumann na nGaedheal were in power after the Civil War, and again in 1934 when de Valera takes over after the election in 1933. These are to give pensions to people who were active in 1916, the War of Independence and eventually the Civil War, and to get those pensions they had to, in some cases, do a question-and-answer session where, again, you're hearing things in their own voice telling you what happened and what they did, or filling out quite detailed forms to explain what happened.

T: Did they have to prove something to get the pension?

CC: They did. They had to get references from three reputable people, and that could be hard to do. The pensions referees, the people who did the granting of the pensions, set up a whole lot of material they sent out in the 1930s, for example, to every surviving head of a unit from the old IRA from the period to know who was there at such and such a date, what were their names, how did they do, what actions were they engaged in on maps, and those are called the brigade activity reports. They went online.

Again, all this is free to access, and they're a huge thing, because if you're from County Tipperary, you go in there and you read through the brigade activity reports, you get down to your local area and you can see exactly what went on during that time. That then will link you into the individual applications for pensions.

It's a pocket social history of certain people in Ireland at that time – how were they fixed financially, where were they living, how were the children being educated? So it's an absolute treasure trove and it's a whole new window. That's what I mean by 'more information'. We're getting stuff that we never had before that was kept locked up because everyone was afraid of it. So the more that comes out, the less afraid we get, the more we can look at it. There could still be rows.

When I was working in Dublin Castle, which was part of the National Archives in the 1970s – I was banished over there from the Four Courts because I was a union activist and I was causing trouble and they thought they could get rid of me, so I had my own little empire there, it was lovely. There was a table where eight scholars could sit. And people kept falling in love over the table because they were so close to each other. It was delightful to watch these romances blossoming.

T: But you were having none of that?

CC: I was delighted! A big, tall priest came in one day from Kerry and he said, 'I need to see everything about the 1798 rebellion from Kerry.' I said there wasn't much going on in Kerry during 1798 and he said, 'Well, there was certain things and I need to see it,' and I said, 'What's your problem? Like, what do you want to find out?' 'There's one gang of people accusing another gang of people of informing on them in 1798.' I said, 'Grand, here's the catalogue, this man will get you the papers.'

He sat there for three weeks. He made copies of everything, goes off satisfied down to Kerry, and is back again a month later, and I said, 'What's wrong? Sure you had all the answers,' and he said, 'Now they've moved on to the Tithe War,' and I said, 'Father, they don't want to be sorted out. They're enjoying the grumbling. It's grand.'

There'll always be that, but for most of us, what we need to know is good, solid evidence-backed information about our past and indeed our present. We all know the expression 'fake news'. We hear it from a certain orange, huge person in the White House, regularly directed at very reputable organizations like the *Washington Post* and *The New York Times*. Fake news is a very dangerous thing because what it means is opinion supplants fact. The most important question any informed human being can ask another human being is: *How do you know what you know?* How do you know that the American government blew up the Twin Towers in 9/11 – one of the most famous conspiracy theories we've had in a long time. You've got to be able to prove it. It's an outrageous claim. Prove it if you think you can say it.

Pubs are dangerously full of this kind of chat all the time. And I hope I'm not offending anyone by saying this among people who are opposed to vaccination – this is a terrible threat to one of the great, gigantic public health successes the human race has ever invented, that has cured terrible childhood diseases like measles and diphtheria. And people are saying, 'No, no, you can't do it.' And I understand people's fears about things, but there is no evidence.

We have to be used to asking for evidence for assertions that people make and to know ourselves what the tools are for testing that evidence. That's what history teaches us.

T: Does it mean us becoming responsible and to look at the past and say it's more complicated than any simple narrative and we have to be responsible and mature in how we react to our history?

CC: Yes, thank you. That's a perfect set of slogans we just got there. I hope that the people who are in charge of the decade of centenaries heard all that and will write it down and make it part of the manifesto for the next few years. That's exactly what we need.

What's interesting is that when people start to engage in local history, in the history of their own area, they get very engaged with it and they get very fascinated by the different characters and personalities that they're coming across, particularly if they knew some of them. If they were kids and these people were older or whatever. That changes your view of things that you start to see, outside your family, first of all. Then, maybe outside your village or the small area that you live in. Then on to who was in charge of what, where, what's the system that runs this small town, for example, who owns the land, who works on the land, what are the institutions nearby, do we have a mental hospital, was there a workhouse, was there a Magdalene laundry, was there a mother-and-baby home, was there a police station, all of these things that make up the system that operates at a given time in a place – look at them. Who's got the money? Who are the businesspeople in the town? What are they doing?

Tom Murphy, who was a great friend of mine, wrote wonderfully about these matters. Tuam was his hometown, and of course so much came from his experience of that as a young man. But again, he understood that the underbelly of what we see in rural Ireland can be very disturbing and dark, as well as with the potential for an enormous amount of love and affection and compassion with good behaviour.

T: Looking back in the way you do, we're kind of leaning towards the strife, if you like, in terms of the stories, but are there joyous things you discover? Is there stuff that makes you laugh?

CC: Absolutely, all the time. I'm a Joyce fanatic. I love James Joyce. Dublin is my city and it was his city. And he used to say if the city was bombed to pieces tomorrow, it could be reconstructed from *Ulysses*, which is partly true. The detail in that book is so wonderful, and if *Ulysses* is too much, read *Dubliners* – anybody who's from Dublin and every Dubliner should read that book because it's our book for our city.

Joyce left Ireland in 1904 with his beloved Nora Barnacle, who he didn't marry for many, many years after it, thus blazing a trail for cohabitation for a lot of people, and fair play to him, she was a wonderful woman. So when I was in the archives, next door to me was a project called Documents on Irish Foreign Policy, which I was one of the editors [of] and a wonderful man called Michael Kennedy was the executive editor. One day he comes into me and he says, 'Catriona, I just found a letter from James Joyce.' I said, 'My God, fab.' So he produces this letter and it's a letter written very shortly before he died in [January] 1941, and he and Nora are travelling from the south of France to Switzerland, where they're going to be safe, because southern France is occupied by the Germans at that point. And he's trying to get his daughter Lucia out of France and into a mental hospital – she was deeply troubled all her life – and he wants Sean Murphy, the Irish ambassador, to help him, and the letter is in green ink. So I had my copy of Richard Ellmann's biography of Joyce handy, and I said, 'Let's see what was going on just then.' So we opened it up on the dates – I think it was December, 1940 – and it has a piece of writing saying Nora opened up the suitcase in which their clothes were, and said, 'Oh my God, Jim, that blessed green ink is all over everything in this suitcase.' I just fell on the floor and laughed. This was the very green ink looking at us all those years later.

And my favourite census return is the Cullens of Blessington Street, Mr and Mrs Cullen, and their four ambitious daughters; one of them is a typewriter, that's what they were called then, there was a bookbinder, and there were two more. And then the last member of the family is 'Tatters Cullen', aged four, place of birth County Longford, relationship to family: dog! They put their dog in the census! So I keep telling people, put your pets in the census, for God's sake, in a hundred years' time you'll give such joy and delight to everybody.

T: What was the average-sized family in the early 1900s?

CC: Now you're treating me as if I'm a historian. I'm not. I'm an archivist, so I'm not going to have at my fingertips statistics and stuff like that. 'Big' is the answer to that. Too big.

T: Do you have a sense of the type of ritual, the type of celebration, the type of commemoration that we should aim for for '21 and '22?

CC: I'm not that keen on commemoration, to be honest with you. I think commemoration of violent periods is not a great idea. I think what you do is you let local people commemorate the events that they want to commemorate in the areas where it's important. That has worked very well in the centenary of 1916, [even though] we did have a state commemoration. Obviously, in 1922, to mark the departure of the British Army and the establishment of the Irish Free State.

Whether we're going to get into the whole business of particular battles, you begin to get into trouble there. Soloheadbeg was the beginning of the War of Independence – Dan Breen and his cohorts shot two policemen in 1919. The state didn't get involved in that. They allowed the local community to commemorate that event, which they did so incredibly respectfully, by inviting the descendants of the two policemen who were unarmed. We have to remember Dan Breen had no permission from anybody to carry that out. He just made up his own mind to do it. It didn't please people in the first Dáil at the time, who were trying to travel a different path. But that was handled with great respect and there was no triumphalism and none of that stuff.

I think it was a huge mistake on the part of the Department of Justice to want to have a big commemoration in Dublin Castle for the RIC.* Don't be doing that. You know, there is a very good organization for former policemen that can look after all of that stuff themselves and do it with great dignity and respect.

What amazed me, though, was how certain a lot of people

---

* The Royal Irish Constabulary, the Irish police force before the establishment of An Garda Síochána.

were that, had they been alive in 1919 or 1920, that they certainly would never have been an RIC man – they might have been. That if they had been, that they would have left immediately and gone and joined the lads in the hills – do we know they would? No. If they'd had a wife and children, that would have been as nought to them? Fine – so Ireland is more important than your family.

We have to think ourselves back into people's minds at the time and what they saw their world as, and not read history backwards, which is very, very common – to look at history from where we are now and not to think, well, actually, there were loads of things they didn't know then.

Nobody foresees the future. We do not know now where we're going to be in three or four years' time. We don't know what is going to happen to us. Things have happened in my lifetime that I never expected, and that was the same for them. So a kind of empathy, particularly with those with whom we might not agree now, is very important.

T: I think that there is a difference between acknowledging and commemorating.

CC: There is. I like the terms 'reflection' and 'interrogation'. I think we need to reflect on what happened and we need to interrogate it, by which I mean: good scholars, find out what happened, look at the archives, look at all of that.

Christy Dignam

'I remember looking at [my new-born daughter]
and thinking, how am I going to look after her in this
world when I can't even make sense of it myself?'

Tommy: It's a pleasure to meet you, fella.

Christy Dignam: I said to myself on the way out, 'Right, I'm dying of cancer, this **** has his work cut out for him today!'

T: Well, just in terms of dying of cancer – will we get through the interview? Are you on the clock?

CD: It depends!

T: What stage are you at?

CD: I'm at the shitting-bricks stage. I've two different types of cancer – multiple myeloma and amyloidosis. They're terminal. But, the vibe is I did chemo three years ago and the chemo's kind of holding it at bay, but it'll come back eventually and then you've to do the whole chemo thing again.

T: And how are ya?

CD: I'm great. I don't feel any different. I just don't think about it, Tommy, you know? It's not something that you want to be thinking about all the time. It would drive you mad.

T: The prospect of death . . .

CD: It's 'there'. It's imminent. Everyone is going to die, aren't they?

T: When you were being treated for heroin addiction, didn't you go to Thailand?

CD: I did, a place called Thamkrabok in the north of Thailand in the middle of a jungle. It's a Buddhist monastery. When you get there, they take all your clothes and your passport and your money and stuff like that. They give you a little uniform to wear and this monopoly money, which is the currency for the actual compound you're on. Every day you come out of your dorm at five o'clock and they have this little drink in a little cup. There's about twenty addicts and they'll be all kneeling by this little kerb with a stream going through it. We'd all kneel down and drink this stuff, followed by a load of water. Then about five minutes later, you start projectile vomiting – it's getting all the toxins out of your system. Fairly hard-core.

T: Where does the Buddhist thing come from in terms of the treatment?

CD: It's more or less just from the goodness of their hearts that they're doing it. The actual compound that they give you to drink was actually made up by a Buddhist in the monastery. It's just like the way the nuns over here would have an orphanage. It's the same deal, they're trying to do something good.

T: Was it hard to get into this place?

CD: It was harder to leave it.

T: I went to a Buddhist retreat recently as well. It was a ten-day silent retreat.

CD: I'd say that was hard for you!

T: At the end of it, I started speaking again and said, 'Ah, I'm still an idiot!' But part of the Buddhist way of thinking is the impermanence of everything, that everything you see has a lifespan. If the world is a single living organism, it has a lifespan. You're saying that, with the cancer, you don't want to think about death, but with the Buddhist thing it's like we're all here for a short time.

CD: Yeah, well, obviously, I think about it. When I go to bed at night, I obviously think about it – you don't want to go tomorrow, you know? You want to try to elongate it as much as you can. But I suppose the Buddhist thing gave me an acceptance of death . . . is this a comedy show?

T: I think it is – did they tell you that's what this was?

T: When you were writing 'Crazy World', who were you thinking about?

CD: My daughter was born in the Rotunda Hospital, and at the time I was strung out. At that time they pulled a curtain around you. There were about eight different beds, a load of babies born at the same time. So they took the baby and brought her off to wash her and they put her in a crib, and I remember when I came out, there were about eight babies there and she shone out. She stood out for me, like, obviously, it's the same for every father. But my wife said to me at the time, 'Look, you've responsibilities now, you'd want to snap out of the buzz you're on.' And I remember looking at her and thinking, how am I going to look after her in this world when I can't even make sense of it myself?

T: It's such an amazing lyric. Can you speak it for us?

CD: 'How can I protect you in this crazy world?'

T: What's the rest of it?

CD: 'I have fallen down so many times, don't know why, don't know where, don't care less, it's all the same. I have travelled through so many towns, don't care less, it's all the same. And how can I protect you in this crazy world? Can you hear the sound of nothing, nothing right, nothing wrong, don't care less, it's all the same. Love is blind, love is real, don't you know that love is what you feel? It's all right, yeah. It's all right. And when the talking's over, and all the crowd have gone. Nothing less we can do, am I ever gonna get through to you? It's all right, so how can I protect you in this craziness.'

T: There ya go.

CD: It's funny, you know? I'll tell you a story about that song. When you're releasing singles, ideally what you want to do is have three singles on the album. You want at least your worst single first, so that'll go to top thirty. Your second best next, that will go top fifteen, and then your latest one, hopefully will go top ten. So we had three songs – 'Crazy World', a song called 'Rainman' and a song called 'Where's the Sun?'. So we were looking at the three songs and we say, 'Right, the one that's the shittiest is "Crazy World" so we'll release that first.' So, we released it and it was a big success! I remember thinking, if they think that's good, wait until they hear 'Rainman'. So, we lashed that out and, I swear to Jesus . . . it kind of taught me you never know what's going to connect with people. It would be the same as you thinking of something that's really funny and you go out to an audience and they just look at you.

T: Do you have a sense of this weight on you, this reality of dying being very present for you? When you look back at your life and the stuff that's happened to you and the impact that you've had with us, like, do you feel like you did the best you could?

CD: Absolutely, yeah. People say, 'You should have done this, you should have been here, and you should have had this success.' But I came from a really poor family in Finglas. I remember when we were kids going to a soup kitchen with my ma – I mean, they're back around Dublin now. We used to get a bowl of stew and a piece of batch bread for a penny at the time. There were eight kids in our family and my father was the only one working, so you come from that. And looking at all of these bands growing up at the time, all I ever wanted to be was a singer. I didn't really care about school because I thought, it's not going to matter, I'm gonna be a singer. I don't measure success in commercial returns, I measure it in the quality of work that you put out there. So I remember thinking years ago, in fifty years' time, let's say, when people are looking at Boyzone's stuff – now I'm not picking on Boyzone particularly . . .

T: But we should!

CD: . . . They're going to look at that stuff and then look at Aslan stuff, and I think people are going to see the quality of our stuff. Even though they had more success and they're much richer than we are, I don't really care about. We've written two songs – 'Crazy World' and 'This Is' – that will go down in Irish history as really, really good songs. Obviously, I'd love loads of money, I still have a big mortgage and all that. And that's something I worry about, because I don't want my wife to be struggling after I go.

CD: To me, it's the difference between success and – not 'failure' – but *non-success*, let's say. It can be the most insignificant little thing. The Cranberries, for example, or The Corrs, the way they took off was just one person seeing it and . . .

T: Yeah, but that kind of success, it flares up and it flares down, and it comes and it goes. What you've managed to do is somehow register those two songs that you mentioned in our DNA. They're part of our bloodstream now in popular culture. For a singer to do that once is a blessing. To do it twice, is . . . two blessings!

CD: If I do it again, how many blessings would that be?

T: That would be . . . more than two anyway!

CD: It's lovely that you would say that.

T: You're so loved, Christy.

CD: To me, that means more than the money. If you'd gone to the eighteen-year-old Christy Dignam and said, 'With the band you have, you can either write two really great songs that are going to go down in Irish history, or you can cover a load of other people's songs and make loads of money but never write anything yourself,' I would have picked the life I got.

T: For sure.

CD: That's all I really care about. I'm not going to be a bullshitter here and say the money doesn't mean anything because, obviously, it means something, you know? I'd love to be rich, but it's not something that I went out after. That wasn't my agenda. In fact, when I started the band, it was during the whole punk ethos, so it was against all that, you know what I mean? It was against commerciality and people abusing musicians and stuff. So, you know, I got what I asked for, unfortunately.

T: How often a week would you sing?

CD: Every day. Every day. I studied bel canto singing for twelve years. It's what Pavarotti sang and studied. I love singing so much that I opened a singing school about four years ago and started teaching kids the proper way of singing. Then I got ill so I had to close the whole thing down. But I still have one student that I kept and I still see him every Wednesday. He comes up to me at eleven o'clock and I give him a lesson because I just love it. I love listening to classical singing, opera. There's times you can't listen to rock 'n' roll – it's too noisy or whatever. But classical music you can listen to at any time. The likes of 'Nessun Dorma' being sung by Pavarotti – no matter what humour you're in, it just stirs you.

T: And could you throw a shape on something like that?

CD: Absolutely – do you want me to give it a lash?

T: Go on.

CD: Can I stand up?

T: You can do whatever you want, fella.

CD [*singing*]:

> *Ave Maria*
> *Gratia plena*
> *Maria, gratia plena*
> *Maria, gratia plena*
> *Ave, ave dominus*
> *Dominus tecum*
> *Benedicta tu in mulieribus*
> *Et benedictus*
> *Et benedictus fructus ventris*
> *Ventris tuae, Jesus*
> *Ave Maria*

Ciara-Beth Ní Ghríofa

'Every single person in this room, theoretically, is on the autism spectrum. There's parts of my story that everyone relates to.'

Tommy: So Ciara . . .

Ciara-Beth Ní Ghríofa: Ciara-Beth. Two names. I'm just that important.

T: All right. OK. What do you do, now? How would I know you?

CNG: So, you probably actually wouldn't know me.

T: I think that's a definite 'yes'!

CNG: Going by the look on your face! So, I'm Ciara-Beth. I'm nineteen years old and I'm on a mission to prove to the world that autism doesn't define a person. At the moment, I'm working on an app to help kids with autism learn to make and maintain eye contact in a way that's comfortable for them.

T: Why is eye contact so important for autistic people, or for anybody?

CNG: For anybody, it's important. I myself was diagnosed with autism when I was fourteen years old. A lot of people say it's a late diagnosis, I say it was an on-time diagnosis. But when I was diagnosed, I kind of had an identity crisis because autism is one of these disorders that comes with a very, very long list of symptoms that can be confused with having a personality. I kind of lost myself a little bit so I decided I'd do what any fourteen-year-old girl would do.

T: Have a baby?

CNG: No! I decided I was going to read all of the academic journals I could find. I read and read and read, and I came across alarming statistics about how a lot of employers said they wouldn't employ somebody if they weren't making eye contact. And then I came across a lot of other studies that were saying that people with autism are frequently underemployed or unemployed, when the vast majority of those of us who are capable of working actually want to be at work. It's not a case that we're too lazy, it's a case that people won't hire us. And so I decided I didn't like any of the statistics I was reading and I was going to do something to change them.

T: What was behind the diagnosis? Like, why were you tested?

CNG: I was always a bit strange. From the age of about eight, we knew there were a lot of red flags that something wasn't quite right. And so I started seeing a lot of different doctors and occupational therapists. I had a brilliant team, in fairness to them. And then it just kind of came by almost a process of elimination, but it was also the best fit. So I assume the doctors knew what they were doing.

T: But isn't autism so broad?

CNG: Ridiculously so, and to the point where I've been told by complete strangers that I can't have autism because I'm a girl, I can talk, I am independent. And I've had people ask me if I'm vaccine-injured, which is a complete myth. People kind of have a lot of assumptions about autism but, in reality, no two people with autism are the same and anything that I talk about is very much my experience and my story.

T: Do you have a sense of loss because somebody has told you you're autistic?

CNG: Not in the slightest. Like, the way I look at it is I was given a diagnosis on a Thursday – I was the same person on the Wednesday and I was the same person on the Friday. It just so happened that I had a label that now explained a lot of difficulties I was having. Every single person that you meet on this earth has some sort of challenge. It just so happens that mine has a name.

T: Can I ask you about the things that were red flags in terms of behaviour or habits?

CNG: Yeah, so, as Irish people, we use a lot of sarcasm and a lot of metaphors and similes. So you know the way you'll say, 'Oh, it's raining cats and dogs outside.' My brain thinks, oh my gosh, those poor animals, in that I take a very, very literal meaning to every word said to me. In some of the cases, it's become more obvious, so, like, I have learned that 'it's raining cats and dogs' means it's just raining quite heavily. But other things, though, like in the back of the classroom, when the teacher is giving out to the entire class because she's not allowed to give out to that one student. I would take that very personally. Because she's not naming the one person, I'm thinking, oh my gosh, she's saying we all have to do better in the homework! So my best was obviously not good enough when, in reality, it's about a select group of students.

And I've a lot of sensory issues. Really loud sudden noises and my brain are not friends. And when I'm confronted with certain sensory triggers, so, like certain textures of clothing, school uniforms, those awful wool jumpers they make you wear, I couldn't wear one. I had a sweatshirt with the school crest on it instead because my skin just could not tolerate the texture. When these things come into play, I have meltdowns which look like a tantrum. And for all intents and purposes, from the outside, it's very difficult to tell the difference. The big difference is that someone who's having a tantrum is not getting their way and can choose to stop. If I'm having a meltdown, it's not voluntary. I am not enjoying it and I'm not benefiting from it in any way, shape or form.

T: It's kind of a panic, isn't it?

CNG: It is. It's very similar to a panic attack. Similar but different.

T: Was it difficult for your family to accept that you had autism?

CNG: I got quite lucky in that my parents obviously knew there was a problem. They wouldn't have brought me to the doctor if there wasn't. I think it was just a great sense of relief that we could actually do things to help. Like, there was no sense of disowning or 'oh my gosh, she's a completely different human being,' it was, 'OK, we have this, where do we go next?' I was always bullied a lot from the age of six to about sixteen. Constant tormenting – people would steal things from me, I had phones go missing, I was hit across the back of the head with water bottles. For a very long time I actually was afraid of going to school, not because of physical violence but because of just how isolated I felt.

Funnily enough, I found a great sense of comfort in the diagnosis because for a long time I had just been told by people in my class, 'Oh, you're just strange, you're just weird, you're just a dork.' Then this magical word came into my life and explained everything, and I was, like, 'I'm not different, I'm just different!' And that's a very difficult concept to explain to teenagers and kids, which is why a lot of the work

I do now is advocacy. Obviously, I'm working on the app, but I go to a lot of conferences and I talk with teachers, student groups, people who work in HR, about diversity and inclusion. I go and I'll either tell my story and explain why autism is not something we should be afraid of, or I go and I explain how easy it actually is to have us involved in your organization or your classroom.

T: Tell me about the app?

CNG: The app is called *My Contact*. It has a picture of people's faces on it and inside the person's eyes is one of four shapes and across the bottom of the screen are four buttons with four different shapes on it, and it's very simply a basic matching game. And the idea that I have behind it – whether or not it's theoretically sound or not is a different debate – is that the person is so focused on having fun matching the shapes that they're being subconsciously desensitized to looking at a person's face or eyes.

T: So it makes it easier?

CNG: Ideally.

T: When you're talking about being bullied, it sounds like an awful thing for a young girl to have to go through.

CNG: I think if it hadn't happened, I'd be a very different person. I wouldn't be sitting here in front of these lovely people talking to you about my story. I'd be a much less interesting person, I wouldn't have learned a lot of skills that I needed to learn, I wouldn't have developed a thick skin, I wouldn't have come up with the ideas, I wouldn't think the way I think now. The way I look at it is what's happening now is a beautiful thing that came from a bad situation, and yes, there were years of torment and years of misery and it was at some points just a living hell, but then I really came into my own and I found that my way of coping was to help other people and to make sure other people don't go through the same thing.

T: Say I met you now, or somebody met you, do you think that they would, like – I'm very slow to use labels like you're this and I'm that, you know – have a sense from your behaviour that you're wired differently? Everyone's wired differently, but would I know from your behaviour? I don't get a sense off you now that you're any different.

CNG: So the way I always describe it is: it's like when you go into a job interview, you're on your best behaviour. But as time goes on and you get to know the people in the office, you relax and your personality comes through. It's very much the same with me in that to you I don't appear autistic, number one, because there isn't one thing that autism looks like, but also because it's as you get to know me that you see what process my brain goes through daily. It's once we're working on a group project together and my train of thought goes from station A to Z while yours is going from A to G that you see that my brain just works that little bit differently.

T: So is your brain flying?

CNG: Sometimes. Sometimes it's a bit slower. It depends on the context, what's going on, social situations. A lot of the time, it's become almost a running joke with my friends that I don't do sarcasm and am always trying to work out are they being serious or not.

T: You're in the wrong country for that.

CNG: Who are you telling?!

T: So do you have habits then that drain you? Like, do you have to lock the lock thirty times before you leave the house?

CNG: No, that would be more obsessive-compulsive disorder. Autism is more being fairly rigid with our routine. If I don't have a routine or a plan, I get very anxious and it sends me into a very bad place.

T: Even though you've been living with this since you were diagnosed at fourteen?

CNG: I've been living with autism since the day I was born.

T: So how old are you now?

CNG: Nineteen.

T: Nineteen? Jesus, Mary and Joseph . . .

CNG: I don't know whether to be complimented or insulted.

T: It's all compliments on this show. So you still have moments and times of great stress and panic above and beyond what you perceive people who don't have autism go through?

CNG: Autism affects me every single minute of every single day. So from the minute I wake up in the morning, I have a routine. If I oversleep and that routine has to shuffle, that's the start of a very anxious day. I go to a lecture and it's cancelled. Anxiety multiplies and people are not predictable, and this bothers me greatly. I find a lot of comfort in predictability. When there's structure, I'm in a very good place, but the minute something changes – and something changes every day, it's just the nature of life – the anxiety starts to build and the autism starts to kick in. I'm still me, but I'm a more anxious, less settled, not-so-happy version of me.

T: How about relationships?

CNG: Relationships. I don't think there's a single nineteen-year-old on the planet who has relationships worked out. If there is one, could they please give me a clue? I don't even really have a lot of time, between working on the app and doing things like this and going to schools and going to conferences and then actually going to college. I'm trying to fit everything into a very small bubble and then trying to make time for friends and family. Anything beyond that at the moment is beyond my realm of thought.

T: It's not something that bothers you or that you think about?

CNG: I'm pretty young, I like to think. I've got some time to work this bit out.

T: I had the ride when I was sixteen! I didn't know it was the ride at the time but, looking back, it definitely was the ride.

T: Two things. First of all, my sister tells me that to be a man is to be autistic because we like to collect things, we like to be in control, we like to know lots of information about really useless stuff. She said all men are just high-functioning autistic people.

CNG: There is a theory that every single person on the planet is on the spectrum. There's just a point where we draw a line and say, 'No, actually, this is interfering with your life. It's a disorder.' Every single person in this room, theoretically, is on the autism spectrum. There's parts of my story that everyone relates to. Nobody likes when their day is messed up. Nobody likes when they show up to work and a meeting is cancelled but they were planning on getting it out of the way.

T: And how does your panic express itself? Say you're going to college and the lecture has been cancelled. Do you start hyperventilating?

CNG: I used to. Now what happens is it takes longer, the anxiety builds over time and then it'll release in the form of

a meltdown, which, like I said earlier, is basically a complicated tantrum.

T: So shouting and roaring?

CNG: Shouting, roaring, crying. It's scary for everyone
involved – for me and the people who are watching. It's even
scary for those who actually know what's going on because
there's very little you can do. When it's something like a
timetable change, you can't just magically fix the timetable.
Or the other thing is, if I have very intense emotions that I
can't process properly, that'll trigger it, and it's not like you
can remove me from a noisy room – you can't remove me
from my emotions. So it is sometimes just a case of riding
the wave and letting it pass.

T: In the case of the lecture, would you be shouting, 'I
can't believe this lecturer hasn't turned up! What the hell
does he think he's doing?'

CNG: No. So it's very much like a toddler tantrum. I can't
put thoughts into words. It's just pure crying and it's awful . . .
actually, the more I talk about it, I'm, like, 'Jeez, what am I
on?!' But it's tough because it's one of those things where you
don't realize what you have until you've lost it and you don't
realize how reliant you are on your words until you don't
have them any more. And I'm very lucky in that, OK, yes, I
have autism, but I have my words. I can sit here and tell you
what I need and why my brain is different. That's why I stand
up and speak out and explain things, because not everyone is
lucky enough to have a voice. And while my experience is my
experience and it's not true to everyone else's, if I make one
person less stigmatized to autism, that's one person who's
going to be more open to understanding their story.

T: How long does it take you to get to the far side of the
panic? And how do you get to the far side of it?

CNG: It varies. The first rule of thumb is I try to make sure that I have someone from my support network with me most of the time. There's usually, like, a designated person. So in the case of at school or at college, it'll be one of my friends in my class, and they know when it starts because I start. It's a gradual transition sometimes in that I just start to become a little bit less talkative, the words just start to become one-syllable answers. And then if it's a case of noise or a sensory factor, they usher me away. Otherwise, a solution is always just to squeeze the life out of me in a really tight hug.

T: To be held tightly?

CNG: Yes. I'm just bawling my eyes out and the hug just tells my sensory system that it's OK. My system goes into fight-or-flight – as far as it's concerned, there might as well be a bear standing over there, and the hug just tells my brain there's no bear here, we're not going to get eaten alive in the next ten minutes, we can calm down now. I've also got a series of coping mechanisms that I myself can put in place. So, like, I'll notice that I'll start to feel really, really warm so I'll need to start having a drink of water, and that can calm me down sometimes. Do you remember fidget spinners, which everyone grew to hate in the last twelve months? I have things that are like those but not half as annoying that I use on a regular basis to keep my sensory system in check.

T: In the way that some people with autism would excel at something, do you have something that you've a flair for?

CNG: I seem to have taken to music. And I definitely seem to have taken to talking and not shutting up!

T: You're on the right show for that!

CNG: I know, it's brilliant! Shortly after I was diagnosed, I started going to Foróige in Galway city. They've a fabulous youth café, and on a Thursday evening they have the sound service programme, where you can go in and just be having a bit of craic with music. I'd bring in my fiddle and one of the volunteers would sit there playing the banjo. He'd play a phrase and I'd play it back, and I took to it quite quickly. The other thing is, a lot of people with autism will have a special interest and it's all we will talk about. For me, that actually seems to be autism itself. So I use that interest as kind of a superpower to try and change the world. I'm on a mission to make the world understand that autism doesn't define a person. Yes, it is a part of my definition as a person, it fuels a lot of what I do, it takes a lot of my time, but it is not the only thing I am.

Elizabeth Oakes

'People spend a year organizing and getting ready for their wedding, where two hundred people might see them. Yet when you're dead, you've nothing prepared and there could be two thousand people coming to view you . . . So it's a huge privilege for me to give the person my time and to be able to look after them the way I would look after my own.'

Tommy: Hello, Elizabeth. Now, Elizabeth Oakes . . . who are you?

Elizabeth Oakes: My name is Elizabeth Oakes. I'm actually from Navan and I'm one of the only people in Ireland to have a degree in Mortuary Science.

T: Whereabouts in Navan are you from?

EO: Johnstown. Where are you from?

T: Well, the father's still living in Balreask, just across the little bridge from ye. Is your family there long?

EO: Forever. Born and reared. Have a farm in Johnstown.

T: I knew no Oakes in school.

EO: I'd say I'm definitely a younger vintage than you, to be honest.

T: Well, the cheeky little head on you! That's why I was asking about your father, because I didn't think we were the same age at all.

EO: No, no, definitely not.

T: Either that or I suffer from stress a lot more than you do. Would I have known your father going to school? Jesus Christ, when you're asking a young wan, 'Did I know your father?' that's the end – you're in the endgame then! I don't think I knew your father going to school. Anyway, tell me about Mortuary Science.

EO: So, what Mortuary Science is, it's basically a degree in funeral directing and embalming. I've always been very entrepreneurial. Since the age of eight I always ran and had my own businesses. When I was eight I used to supply rabbits and guinea pigs to the local pet shops in Navan. I grew up on a farm and knew about the birds and the bees. At the height of it I had thirty-six rabbits and eighteen guinea pigs, so it was a full-on business.

T: How did you get the rabbits and guinea pigs to breed?

EO: I bought a boy and a girl!

T: And you knew that . . . ?

EO: Well, growing up on a farm, you kind of know what happens around the place, like. Then I progressed and I bought and sold a couple of ponies, Connemara ponies. And when I went to Mercy Convent in Navan I set up a little tuck shop called Busy Lizzy. As soon as the bell would go I would write down everyone's name and what they wanted in the shop. And the deal was I wouldn't give you any change. And you had to give me at least fifty cents for going. The more that you ordered, the more commission I had to get. I had a deal done then with the nun to say I didn't have to stand in the queue. I just ran in, filled the bag with sweets, she totted up the list and I was back in the classroom within five minutes. I had about ten or fifteen euro in my pocket every day for myself.

It was a great little business. I actually got awards for

attending school. I never missed a day because I was making so much money by just going into school.

T: And did it ever strike you to just buy some sweets and share them with your friends?

EO: That wouldn't have been very entrepreneurial, would it?

T: No.

EO: So, it came to the Leaving Cert and, academically, I probably wouldn't have been the most committed. I was only going to the school because of the business. Our career guidance teacher gave us this FÁS disc at the time. I put it into the computer and I wanted to find a career that was the shortest amount of time in education but where you got the most money in the end. I was going through all this stuff and it said, 'Embalmer – one-year apprenticeship, sixty thousand per annum.' I didn't actually read any further. I didn't even have to have my Leaving Cert; all I needed was an interview. I said, 'This is win-win.'

I went into my mother. She was drying the dishes and I said, 'Mam, you have to ring this number. I have to go and have an interview. I'm going to be an embalmer.' She flicked the towel over her shoulder and rang this number in Mayo, and *plamásed* away, and she said, 'Right, get your stuff ready – we're going down on Saturday.' To Mayo, to a guy called Dave McGowan. I was delighted with life, I hadn't studied up until that anyways in school and now I didn't even have to do the Leaving Cert if I didn't want to. So I went down to Mayo –

T: Was he surprised to see you?

EO: He probably was.

T: Like, was there a queue of people trying to get in the door?

EO: No, I was the only one that turned up! So I had the chat anyway, and he said, 'Right, if this is what you want to do, I'll take you on the course.' I said, 'Brilliant,' and that was the start of it. As soon as I was finished the Leaving Cert I was shipped off to Ballina to start my apprenticeship.

T: In the interview, what did he say was involved?

EO: Well, he said it was like an operation and that you had to be OK with that. I said, 'Look, when I was five I used to lamb a lot of sheep, and there's three things sheep love doing: getting caught in wire, getting stuck on their back and dying, so,' I said. 'I'll be grand.'

T: Jesus!

EO: And he accepted me on the course. At that stage, I had my mind made up and this is what I was going to do. So off I went to Mayo and I started my apprenticeship down there, and I did everything from driving the hearse, digging the grave –

T: You weren't selling sweets on the road as you were . . . ?

EO: And then, obviously, doing the embalming.

T: So, to be an apprentice in embalming, does that mean that you just watched David doing it initially?

EO: Initially, you'd go in and you'd just watch the procedure being done, and then you start getting involved in the technical details of it.

T: What actually is embalming?

EO: Well, embalming is an operation that happens on the dead body. When the blood settles in the body and is no longer being circulated around, what happens is it goes black and it can stain the body. What embalming does, it solidifies the protein in the cells to stop the body from going off or decaying. So, therefore, we remove the blood from the body and we replace that blood with our embalming chemical, which preserves the proteins in the cells.

T: How much fluid is it?

EO: About two gallons.

T: Does it have any other uses?

E: Sheep dip, maybe! No, formaldehyde.

T: It's formaldehyde?

EO: It's formaldehyde, yeah. So, that's basically it and, obviously, we wash the body and we cosmetize, and we would do the hair and put them into their coffin and make sure that they are really appropriately presented to the family.

T: When my mother came back from the mortuary, she didn't look like herself. They just got the make-up slightly wrong. It was strange, because my sisters and my wife saw her and said, 'It doesn't look like Helen at all.' So they got their make-up stuff out and started brushing her up.

EO: A lot of times, I suppose, the undertaker or the mortician is male. So they mightn't have the skills necessary to do the make-up on a woman.

T: So you drain the body of blood and then you put in the formaldehyde. What else do you do?

EO: Well, what can happen again is, obviously, if people are after eating, there can be a lot of gaseous build-up in the intestines, so you've to remove the gaseous build-up. Say, over time, if the gas isn't removed from the intestines, it can get bigger and bigger and it can put pressure on the stomach or on the lungs and the air can come out unexpectedly.

T: So how do you get it out?

EO: It's a special technique that we use.

T: A fartorectory or something, is it? Are you Ireland's only fartologist?

EO: It's just a procedure [using an instrument] called a trocar.

*

EO: It's obviously a very, very important job. People spend a year organizing and getting ready for their wedding, where two hundred people might see them. Yet when you're dead, you've nothing prepared and there could be two thousand people coming to view you. You don't know what you're going to wear or what way you're going to look. So it's a huge privilege for me to give the person my time and to be able to look after them the way I would look after my own.

T: Do you deal with people coming back from accidents?
EO: Yes.
T: And what's that like?
EO: Well, I'm actually much better dealing with dead people than I am with live people. If I know someone is dead, I can cope with the situation. But if I was at a panicked car accident and people were screaming and crying, I wouldn't be good in that situation. So, I suppose, I just feel that it's my responsibility to put this person back together and make them look the best they can so that the family can start a healthy grieving process. When I finished my one-year apprenticeship in Mayo, David said, 'You really have a passion for this.'
T: For the dead?
EO: For the dead! Absolutely! He said, 'You really need to go to America, and you can get a degree in Mortuary Science,' because America is the only place where you can get your degree. My family said, 'We'll be able to pay for your college and everything like that, but you're really going to have to fend for yourself once you get there.'

I enrolled in my college in California, but I had nowhere to live. When I was in fifth and sixth class in school, I used to mind both my grand-aunts. I used to put them on the commode every night and dress them and get them ready for bed. So I was used to minding older people and I remember [thinking], If only I could mind an old person in their own home in lieu of rent, I'd be sorted.

I was actually living in this woman's campervan outside her house. I was staying there until I could find somewhere to live. One day she said to me. 'I've a pass for the gym, do you want to come with me?' I met this couple just by absolute chance called the Murphys – typical American, had never set foot in Ireland but were as Irish as could be. They were so nice to me and they said, 'Is there anything you want or anything you need while you're here?' I said, 'Well, I actually need somewhere to live.'

I went over to their house, and the woman that lived opposite them, her name was Lucile. She was in her mid-eighties, only one block from college, she had a four-bedroom house and lived on her own. We just clicked. It was the best thing that ever happened, like, I had to be accountable for her, she was like my grandmother. I moved in with her that day and we were best friends ever since. She's actually a hundred and four right now. Every month we write letters to one another and I send pictures.

T: What did they teach you in America that you weren't learning in Mayo?

EO: Well, in Mayo it was just an apprenticeship, so you did your course and that was fine. You can be a funeral director and an embalmer. It's a kind of unregulated industry, so you can be a funeral director and embalmer in the morning if you want. When I went over there it was to get that piece of paper to get my degree in Mortuary Science. There was obviously much more entailed – it was a three-year degree course that went through every aspect of funeral directing and embalming. We used to go down to LA county morgue. I remember the first time I went in it was like an acre of a fridge and it was just bodies everywhere, and I was going around looking for toe tags and serial numbers to try and find the ones that we were going to bring back for our lab class.

T: When you walk into a room where there's a body, talk me through that. Do you have music on? Do you listen to the radio?

EO: I actually like chatting to them.

T: What do you say to them?

EO: Well, I'd be chatting to them and it's just, I suppose, I look at the person and I try and figure out what sort of life had they.

T: Give me an example of what you would – say, you walk in . . . ?

EO: I'd say, 'Well, Betty. I'm Elizabeth and I'm going to be looking after you. You don't have to worry, you're in good care now.' And then I start doing my procedure, and that's really how it goes.

T: And would you talk to them while you're doing the procedure?

EO: Ah, yeah, you would because, otherwise, it's . . . I'm a chatter.

T: And there's no fear of interruption! So as you're talking, what're you saying? Say you're doing something with their feet or their legs, what do you say?

EO: The way I think of it, or I suppose the way I've had to think of it, is I feel they're going up to this big party up in the sky and it's my responsibility to get them ready for this party. I'd be saying, 'Now, you're going to meet lots of people up there and I'm going to have you looking lovely. You don't have to worry about anything.' I really do feel that it's a huge responsibility to get this person looking as well as they can for the big party that I feel is up there.

T: Would you ever talk to them about stuff that you're going through?

EO: Ah, well, you might, but you're not going to get any advice, are you?

T: It's amazing. I suppose the rest of us are so scared of bodies. You know when you kiss a corpse, they feel so cold . . .

EO: I know. I always say this, trying to lighten everybody, I say: 'Just like talking about sex won't make you pregnant, talking about death won't make you dead.' Let's start the conversation.

T: What do you think we need to talk about in terms of death?

EO: I do think it's important that people make funeral wishes. It can definitely lessen the grief process and it can put people into a different mode when a death occurs if the person who is deceased has even a song that they like or if they want to be buried or cremated. It can make a huge difference to the family that's left behind. It's inevitable: we're all going to die. And it is probably the most significant event that's going to happen in our lives, yet we have no control over it. That's something that I would definitely advocate: start talking about what you would like for your end-of-life options.

T: Is that because you've seen funerals where no decision has been made and what has happened because no decision has been made?

EO: Well, it can cause a lot of tension within families, it can cause feuds, and that's why it is important that people know what people want.

T: When? Like, I'm fifty.

EO: I'd be starting to make your arrangements!

EO: When I came back from America, I was kind of very young and the industry didn't take me very seriously and it was the time of the recession. So when I was over there I did take another course. It was a two-day course which was permanent make-up, tattooing eyebrows.

T: Two days? That's fairly thorough!

EO: I know, for tattooing on eyebrows and eyeliner. When I came home, I was lucky that I had that course behind me as well. The funeral industry wouldn't take me seriously and it was a very hard thing to penetrate. So I pursued a career in the permanent make-up field then. I always stayed current within the funeral industry. About two years ago, I attended a convention and I came upon this technology which is a sustainable, environmentally friendly alternative to flame cremation and burial. It's actually cremation through water instead of flame. I was shortlisted for Ireland's Best Young Entrepreneur of the Year with my business start-up idea. We're hoping to have that open in 2020.

T: How does that work through water?

EO: There's a stainless-steel vessel. The body is wrapped in a woollen shroud –

T: Just like Jesus!

EO: Yeah. And placed within the vessel. And what happens is, it's a solution made up of 95 per cent water and 5 per cent alkaline, and that's washed over the body and it dissolves all the soft tissue, so what remains then are the bones. The bones are then taken out and put into a cremulator; it's the same as with flame cremation.

T: Is that a thing – that's not a Nespresso?

EO: No, it's more like a food processor. They're processed down to the dust, then that's what the family receive as their loved one's ash. It's an environmental alternative because in cremation, obviously there's a lot of CO_2 released. With flame cremation, the skin is burnt and the flesh is burnt off the body. And when I worked as a cremation operator in America, you rake the ashes, so you rake the bones to the front and they fall into a steel bucket and they have to be let cool because they're very hot. Then you run a magnet over the body, and any hips or anything like that are taken out, and then the bones are placed into the cremulator and processed down to the dust that the family receive back.

T: What is it that attracts you to the dead?

EO: It's just that I love helping people in their time of need. I feel the funeral is more for the living than for the dead. Even in my permanent make-up career, I'm dealing with a lot of people who may have stage 4 cancer and are in these very traumatic situations. I just love to be able to give back to those people. That's what makes me want to progress.

T: Tell me, what does a funeral director do?

EO: Well, obviously, they direct funerals. They do everything from start to finish. It's not every day that someone is organizing a funeral, so they don't know what to do when somebody actually dies. That's where the funeral director steps in. In Ireland, it's only a two-day event, which is a very fast turnaround time. Whereas in England, it's a month sometimes. So a funeral director, it's their place to make sure that everything runs smoothly and that the family are looked after, and it can definitely help with the grieving once that's facilitated at a proper level.

T: What can you tell us about the way that Irish people are dying now?

EO: Well, I personally feel that death has become very medicalized. You have women or men, and they're eighty-nine and they've lived a very full and healthy life, and they die but the family want to resuscitate them and then maybe have them in a vegetative state for God knows how long. I think death has become taboo and it's nearly like a medical misadventure when somebody dies.

Like having a baby, there's actually a process involved in dying. There's a process that people go through, the stages that they go through before they die, and again it is a natural process that happens. But I think medicine has come in and has probably kept people alive maybe in uncomfortable states. Maybe their time should have been shortened a little bit. But that's hard for even me to say because if someone belonging to me was dying, I would want to keep them for as long as possible.

T: Do you think some families are better at dealing with death than others?

EO: Absolutely. If somebody has a long-drawn-out illness and it's expected – it's funny, some people are still shocked when it happens. If it's a very sudden death, obviously it's terrible and it's very hard for everyone to deal with.

T: I was very grateful when my mother died. Paddy Fitzsimons in Navan, the way himself and his family [handled it]. One of the things I really enjoyed was the pageantry of it. So as the coffin was making its way from the removal home to the church, Paddy walked out in front of the hearse dressed in black with a big black top hat, and he kind of strolled out and he stopped the traffic. The hearse went down Trimgate Street and it was like this woman's death was an event that

the town had to stop for. And I remember as a young fella –
and I presume it still happens now, no matter where you
were or what you were doing, if a hearse was driving past
you'd stop and you'd take off your hat or whatever and you'd
let them go. I've always been very grateful for Paddy's pageantry as my mother was being buried. It was fantastic.

EO: Definitely, in Ireland, we do death well. Even the
whole wake, people coming to the house – people need that
healthy and supportive safe place to grieve where they can
have their outpours of emotion and know that people understand it.

T: What's the funniest thing you've ever seen at a funeral
or a removal?

EO: I remember we had a contract for anybody who died
off the coast. So, it was this young, very handsome man who
had died. He was Spanish; Pedro, I think, was his name. It
was my responsibility to look after him. He had no clothes or
anything, so they had these [burial] habits – you know the
frilly Victorian neck and a big picture of Mary on the front
of it and it's pure shiny? I just looked at this handsome man
and thought, Oh my God, this is not happening!

T: Down to JD Sports or something?

EO: Up to St Vincent de Paul! I took his measurements
and I got him socks, jocks, suit, shirt – the whole nine yards.
He looked absolutely amazing being sent off. I'd say when
the family seen him, they said, 'Where is he after coming
from?'

T: So over the next short while you'll be hoping that the
water-based crematorium idea – that that takes off?

EO: That's the big picture, and I definitely think it's going
to revolutionize the industry as a whole. It's not very often
that younger people – female – enter this industry, and I just

really feel, with the green agenda, with the reach I have on social media, that the time is right, my voice will be heard.

T: I get a great sense of care off you and I think it's obvious to anybody listening to you, your care for the people who are grieving but also to respect the sanctity of the person who has just died.

Ifrah Ahmed

*'It's just like cutting yourself and putting lemon or
even perfume on it, that is the kind of feeling I had. And
that's why I risk my life to do something now – I want to
make it so that those young girls don't feel the pain I've
been through or what has happened to me.'*

Tommy: Ifrah.

   Ifrah Ahmed: Yes.

   T: Where are you from?

   IA: I'm from Drumcondra.

   T: I thought I recognized the accent!

   IA: I came to Ireland back in 2006.

   T: . . . From?

   IA: Guess where I'm from.

   T: Somewhere in Africa? Don't be getting annoyed at me now! Sierra Leone.

   IA: No.

   T: This could take a while . . .

   IA: Two more guesses.

   T: Are you from Liberia?

   IA: Do I look like I'm from Liberia?

   T: Don't take that attitude with me, missy! Congo?

   IA: Forget about it. I'm from Dublin. Drumcondra. And I now live in the place where you got married – Monaghan.

   T: I thought I detected a trace of that accent too!

IA: I was nearly eighteen years old when I came here. So I'll tell you where I'm from – I'm from Somalia originally. But I'm a very proud Irish citizen.

T: Well, we're delighted to have you. I mean that.

IA: Thank you.

T: Why did you come from Somalia?

IA: Basically, Somalia has been at war over thirty years. I came to Ireland as a refugee. I was one of the luckiest people and was received in Ireland very well. I was given welcome and I was given refugee status and now I have an Irish passport. Then I started campaigning against the practice of female genital mutilation. Do you know what that is?

T: I have a very rough idea.

IA: Somalia is one of the countries where female circumcision is practised and it is practised by 98 per cent of the population there. When I came to Ireland first, I went to hospital. As an African refugee asylum-seeker, you have to go through a medical check like every other asylum-seeker, a test for Aids, hepatitis, you name it, that people think African people have. But when I was taken to hospital for these tests, there was one thing that I found Ireland had no clue about and the medical team were very ignorant about, and that was female circumcision. It had been done to me when I was eight years old. So when they gave me a smear test and one of the nurses asked me what happened to me, I was shocked and I was so angry and annoyed because I felt, why don't you know that this is my culture?

I felt that female genital mutilation was something that we have to explain to Irish society. I went back to the asylum centre where I was with another eighteen young refugees and I asked them was it the same as my experience and they all said it was. I told them that somebody had to speak out.

The girls refused because they said, 'We are refugees, we don't understand this language, we don't want to get into trouble.' So I took the lead and said I will speak out.

I didn't know what a smear test was and the worst thing was that my translator was a man who I was telling my personal experience of female circumcision to. And it was very shameful for me to speak to a man about this. So I started campaigning within Ireland. I felt that was something that Irish people had to understand because there are young girls who are born in Ireland that are at risk.

I became very friendly with the Labour Party, who took the issue on board, and after six years the Female Genital Mutilation Bill was passed in Ireland and it became a law. Then I decided to continue my campaign so that I could have my voice heard around the world and I became a European activist because my Irish citizenship allows me to travel. I risked my life going back to Somalia in 2013 because I felt I could give back to the community. When I first went, I found young girls being subjected to rape and different sexual violence, and also child marriage and female genital mutilation. I remember when I was given my status in Ireland as a refugee, the first thing I was told was I had a voice and I had a right to leave. I was given a voice in Ireland and with that voice I went to use it in Somalia.

T: Could you explain to me exactly what female circumcision is?

IA: Female circumcision is basically cutting young girls age zero to twelve years, and they remove all of the clitoris and sew everything back up again. It causes death, kidney infections, different diseases, and a mother giving birth to a child is at risk of death from bleeding. And also, there is a culture in Somali men that if he takes the woman to hospital, then he is not a man. If he uses his power to open the lady, in that time she can also die from bleeding. It really damages the women's life. It is a cultural practice because people believe that it has a religious element, but it doesn't have anything to do with religion. It's a cancer. We were doing a religious and media training in Mogadishu and during our training there was this young girl ten years old. She died in a village because she was cut and that really made me upset. I could not let it go because that girl died. Somalia is not safe. But if I can save one girl's life, I want to be there.

T: Can I ask you what reason do people give for mutilation?

IA: It's different because some people, they say it's religion and it has to be practised because they believe that.

T: What religion?

IA: Islam. And female genital mutilation has no place in Islam or any other religion. It is a barbaric cultural practice.

T: What's the relationship between Somali people and sex, in terms of sexual relations between men and women? Is it seen as something for both people to enjoy?

IA: The first thing they say about female genital mutilation is that it protects the young girl. The family believe that if the girl is not cut, then she can go and have sex with everyone. That is what they believe, because there are lots of women around the world who are not cut who are still living their life and having these sex lifestyles. I come from a place where people don't talk about sexuality and people don't talk about even female genital mutilation. I was not really allowed to talk about it even living in Ireland. I used to get blackmailed and a lot of people threatening that they were going to kill me. They were going to shut my mouth if I don't stop talking about it.

In our culture there is no place that people talk about sexuality openly. Women who are circumcised before they marry are not given an opportunity to speak to their husband in terms of their sexuality and don't disclose about the female genital mutilation because this is the culture. I met with a lot of women who say that the men use them hard and, you know, some of them, they can never have babies.

T: Does the act of it somehow make women ashamed of their vaginas?

IA: Well, it's really hard to say, because that is how God has made us and there's nothing to be ashamed of. For me now, I believe that my grandmother took away something that belonged to me that I can never have back. And when I talk to other girls, they tell me about the clitoris and the feelings they have and all that, and it makes me really upset because we don't have these kinds of feelings. And every time I look at myself, I just feel like, why am I different to a young Irish or non-Somali women who are not cut? And that is one answer I could never get from my family or anyone else. But this is the answer I want to give to young girls who are raised in this country, to feel that nothing is missing in their bodies because someone says that if the clitoris is not cut, you're not clean. And some families say it's because if the girls are not cut, they're not really going to be good because they're going to mess around and have sex with different men. It's not religion, it's culture.

T: The mutilation – how exactly do they do it?

IA: Let me take you back to myself when I was first cut. I remember it was my grandmother's brother who did it to me. And I remember coming into a room where we were, all together, ten girls. There was one scissors and the only thing that they had been doing was washing it with hot water and soap. And then the next person goes through. And I remember one of the other nine girls died because she could not go to the toilet. She was damaged so badly and sewn back together so hard she could not wee. And I remember my grandmother holding my hands and my grandmother's brother was cutting my clitoris and sewing. And there's not even anything to support your pain being given to anybody. It's just like cutting yourself and putting lemon or even perfume on it, that is the kind of feeling I had. And that's why I risk my life to do something now – I want to make it so that those young girls don't feel the pain I've been through or what has happened to me.

I feel my grandmother has damaged me. But I was given an opportunity in Ireland. I was given a better life. This better life, I want to take it back. Before I came to Ireland, I was living with my grandma, and I never seen a problem. But now, as a grown woman, a woman who can live her life the way that she wanted, I went back. I was given the opportunity to live here. I say if I can save one girl's life, I will take that opportunity to fight for it and to continue that fight and say I don't want any other girl to go through what has happened to me. And I want these young girls to be safe from this terrible practice. I'm lucky. I'm really lucky.

T: For our natural inclination to want to protect our daughters, and then to experience that kind of violence . . . Mentally, how does that change you?

IA: I remember being in Ireland, speaking to the community. I was given a hard time and I ran away from Dublin to Drogheda just to be safe. But after a couple of months of living in Drogheda, I realized that I am missing something which is that, for me at least, I'm in a better country where I can go to a doctor and I can tell my pain. I can see a psychiatrist who I can share with all the things I've been through. I can stay here and do what I want to do, but watching those girls, I have to fight back and say what they have been doing to us is wrong and we have to give back those girls [their] life. So that is my strength.

T: There's the barbarity of the act, for somebody so young to be going through that – you can sense here the horror of hearing about this – but in Somalia, does it make any difference?

IA: No, it doesn't. I remember the first time when I went back to Somalia I sat with religious and community leaders, women's and youth groups, and politicians. I was trying to explain about why this practice should stop and how we have to educate those mothers who are practising it. Every time, the message I got back was, 'Go back where you come from, you've been in the Western world too long, you're brainwashed.' I've been in and out of Somalia almost four years now, and these four years have been very hard, because they reject me. In a way, the problem is that Somalia is 100 per cent Muslim communities, so it's basically the religious leaders that sometimes make your life hard. So I went to the Ministry of Women in the Somali government and started working with them.

It's been very hard – I get upset sometimes and I just go, 'OK, I'm going back to Ireland, I don't belong here.' For example, at the end of last year we lost seven girls to female genital mutilation, and there was one particular young girl, her name was Deka. I went to her village to meet with her mother, father, grandfather and grandmother, just to get some answers about why did they do it and why they didn't take her to hospital when they found she was bleeding. But I couldn't get these answers, and the worst thing was that when I went to the hospital, the doctors who received the girl told me, when they asked the father to donate blood, he wouldn't give any blood. Maybe if he had, her life could have been saved.

I have my own foundation called the Ifrah Foundation, and a beautiful Irish team who are supporting my campaign. They sent me money to travel to her village and make a documentary, and that documentary went to all Somali news. Her story went around the world and Somalia. Since then, when a girl is found bleeding for hours, I could get a phone call and can help the contact facilitate calling around and asking hospitals to take this child and support with blood. If the family say they don't have money, I can try to send them money for her treatment. But there are certain areas that the foundation board members won't allow me to travel to and I have to convince them that it's safe for me.

When I was doing that documentary, I never told them who I was because, if you do in some areas, and the people find out that you come from Europe, you have a lot of them saying, 'Give us money, otherwise we will cut more girls.' So I pretended that I was just a normal Somali woman. And then we interviewed mothers about their daughters being saved, and asked them how they became aware that the girls would die if they didn't go to hospital, and they said, 'Oh, we heard about this girl Deka who died and we were scared that our daughters might die too.'

I kept saying, 'OK, if that is the case, why are you still practising FGM?'

If I can save girls by educating mothers, talking to the politicians, talking to anyone, I would do whatever it takes. But in a country that is 100 per cent Muslim, which has been at war for over thirty years, and practises this in the community almost every day, how can you change that mentality?

T: It takes a leader to change a tribe.

IA: That is why we keep going. But then again, if you are not a man, you are nobody. I come from this culture where men are the power and women are no one.

T: Can I ask you how you came from Somalia to Ireland?

IA: I wasn't coming to Ireland, but I'm lucky that I ended up here. I was going to America with a trafficker . . .

T: You came with a trafficker?

IA: Yes.

T: Can you tell me what that was like?

IA: I came alone by bus from Mogadishu to Ethiopia. It was very tough, because there were a lot of military on the street and some of the women were being raped by them. There was also a lot of damage to the bus during our trip. Sometimes daytime is hard to travel so we travelled at night . . .

T: To avoid the military?

IA: Yes, they stop the bus, they take all the money, they take the food, they take everything, and they rape women. I was so lucky because I was very young and the bus driver was very helpful because I was this kid and he could see that I was travelling for the first time myself. And then it was a very hard train journey. Then I meet the trafficker in Addis Ababa, and we flew from Addis to another country in Europe and then we came to Ireland. The trafficker was saying, 'OK, now you're in a safe country because Ireland looks after refugees, so you can start a new life here.' I said OK, but I wasn't OK because I was thinking that I was going to go to America.

After meeting with all these immigrant women around

the world in different conferences, I see that I am lucky that I am from Ireland. I may not have had this opportunity in America or in the UK. I never say I'm from Somalia, I just say I'm from Ireland or from Drumcondra. The truth is that this is where my life began, meeting new people, going to English class. I started a new life but, today, I'm happy to say that I can make a difference to save young girls within the country and outside the country.

T: Can I just say that it's remarkable work that you do and you're a remarkable woman. And I'm very, very proud that you're Irish.

IA: Thank you.

Joanne McNally

*'I remember . . . there was a girl in my school who had an
eating disorder and people were saying, "It's not about
food, it's about control." And I was saying, "Bullshit,
of course it's about her body." I really don't think I
fully understood it until I was about a year into
treatment and the penny dropped.'*

Tommy: So what attracts you to stand-up?

Joanne McNally: Nothing . . . did *you* always want to do
stand-up?

T: Well, I'm not able to do anything else!

JM: A lot of stand-ups say that. I don't believe it.

T: I swear to God! I was on the dole until I was forty-one.

JM: Shut up.

T: Well, twenty-five.

JM: Not the same thing.

T: I genuinely had tried a few different things very unsuc-
cessfully, and I'm not somebody who's very good at doing
stuff that I'm not interested in. If I was born three hundred
years ago, I'd be doing a version of this.

JM: So, I had no interest in stand-up. I'd never actually
been to a stand-up gig in my life. I was working in PR and I
was accidentally cast in a show called *Singlehood* because I
knew the director, and they cast [Irish comedian] P. J. Gal-
lagher and he suggested I do stand-up. I said no, like any

normal person would, and then he said, 'Look, I'm going on tour, you can come on tour with me and learn the ropes that way,' and that's what I did. At the time, I didn't realize what an opportunity it was. My first stand-up gig was in the Hawk's Well Theatre in Sligo.

T: Jesus Christ, what a place to start, like. So your first gig was on a support slot to an established stand-up comedian – that's phenomenal.

JM: No! I was kind of thrown out as the circus act at the start, like the brand-new girl. I think I did five minutes, but I was doing fifteen minutes by the end of the tour.

T: And what did you find yourself talking about when you got onstage? What *do* you talk about?

JM: Well, I started talking about Des Bishop only having one testicle – that was my first gag. It was something about me having numerical dyslexia so when I came back up from going down on him, I'd think he had twelve testicles. Yeah, it worked about as well in Sligo. But yeah, that was what I started with, but when I was doing *Singlehood*, the show, I used to talk about this guy that I'd met. This sounds awful, but when you're in your twenties as a woman, you've one guy who's always trying to get *into* you, you know yourself. I was basically standing onstage giving out about lads, and PJ was basically, like, you could tour that.

T: Do you object to us? What are we doing wrong?

JM: No, it's not that. I like talking about that stuff. It takes a comedian ten years to find their voice, isn't that what they say?

T: I'm doing stand-up twenty-one years now and I still panic as much when I'm putting a show together as I did when I started.

JM: That's good to know. As a female comedian – even

though I hate even identifying as that – I do kind of gravitate towards relationships and sex and things like that.

T: So tell me what you think about relationships and sex.

JM: They give me great material for stand-up. I'm worried if I ever meet anyone I like that I'll have to retire. I talk about Tinder and online dating. So I talk a lot about that kind of stuff, but then I do kind of try and veer off into other kind of areas so that I'm not a one-trick pony. But I always end up coming back to talking about my menstrual cycle. I like it, it gets laughs.

T: Tell us about your menstrual cycle. Is it unusual?

JM: I'm not giving away my gags.

T: How many times a week would you perform?

JM: Fairly regularly. I was sick a long time before I got into stand-up. Basically, I was working in PR and got very sick with eating disorders, bulimia primarily, so I had to leave work and go into treatment. And while I was there, I wrote a lot about it, and then came out of treatment and did *Singlehood*. Because I wasn't working, I allowed myself to start a new career. The illness allowed me that freedom. Then I used what I'd written and wrote a show with a friend of mine, [*Singlehood* director] Una McKevitt, for the Dublin Fringe Festival called *Bite Me*, which we sold out and it was nominated for three awards. I'm going to tour that now.

T: Not knowing much about women or eating disorders, what exactly is bulimia, do you mind me asking?

JM: It's very hard to explain. You'd probably be more familiar with anorexia. I was anorexic-bulimic – I had both. With anorexia, the mindset is to lose weight. With bulimia, the mindset is to maintain, binge and purge, whereas anorexia would just be not eating. But I was caught in this binging and purging but also very underweight and whatever else, so I wrote a comedy show about it.

T: Did the treatment locate the source? Because I'm imagining it's not a physical disease.

JM: Yeah, it was an addiction. So it's like, if you're an alcoholic, you can identify as an alcoholic and you can stop drinking, but what you are doing is just masking all this other shit. So once you stop whatever it is you're doing, that self-destructive thing, then you have to tackle all the reasons why you were doing it, and actually that's the hardest bit, really, it's exhausting. So that took a long time, and I'll manage it for the rest of my life.

T: And when a family member develops something like that, it has consequences for the rest of the family then, does it?

JM: My poor mother. I was living in town on my own and I was functioning as a bulimic for a long time. And then I just stopped. Stopped functioning completely. I wasn't going to work, getting sick all day. So my mum actually had to come into town and take me out of my house and bring me home. I lived with her for two years, but I was still living as someone with an eating disorder. It doesn't just stop because you acknowledge it, so it was very tough on her. And I didn't tell my brother Connor for a long time, but when I eventually did, he was like, 'I know, I've been going to meetings for a long time so that I could support you when you eventually told me.'

But it was really hard. No family is equipped to deal with that stuff. I would say I'm recovered now, but I'd be too scared to laugh in the face of it and say that part of my life is over. If I ever felt myself drifting back into it, I would just go back to treatment.

T: What are the signs of drifting back into it?

JM: I would still sometimes see someone underweight who's probably quite sick and I'd sometimes be like, 'Oh wow, look at their figure,' and then I have to check myself and be like, no, it's very obvious they're not well. But I'll never go back to being sick again. I hope.

T: What's the best way for a family member to deal with somebody in their family who has an issue with food?

JM: So many people do. It's mad. Since I did the show and a lot of press before it, I've had a lot of parents on to me. I was like a crème brûlée – my family and friends just kept tapping at me until eventually I cracked. Because you think what you're doing is the right thing, you think you're on a health kick. You think everyone else is overly concerned or else they're jealous of your new body.

T: And were you getting compliments about your body?

JM: Of course, there's a reward for it. You're controlling and you're getting compliments and you're beginning to look like what you're told you should look like. If you say to someone with an eating disorder, 'You're too thin,' they don't hear you saying, 'You're too thin,' they hear it as a compliment.

What worked for me was friends saying, 'You look really sick, you look really unwell.' You can't tell someone they're too thin, because that just spurs them on. They're achieving what they want to achieve.

T: Is there any wisdom in family members bringing up the subject?

JM: You have to. And it's really hard – like, my family, we killed each other for so long because there's so much denial around it. Like any addiction, you think that they're trying to take away the one thing that's making your life bearable. When I eventually got to a stage where I knew I couldn't live as a bulimic person any more, I bawled crying. I couldn't understand how I'd ever be happy without it. Even though it was ruining my life.

T: Such a strange thing, isn't it, because it's not actually what you look like, it's your attitude to what you look like.

JM: Yeah, but I was convinced. I remember when I was really young and there was a girl in my school who had an eating disorder and people were saying, 'It's not about food, it's about control.' And I was saying, 'Bullshit, of course it's about her body.' I really don't think I fully understood it until I was about a year into treatment and the penny dropped.

T: Have you encountered many men with eating disorders? There's a lot more pressure on men now to have particular types of body.

JM: Not as many, but it's definitely a thing for lads now, yeah. Maybe they're just not saying it. I was lucky in that my eating disorder got so severe that I'd no option but to check out of my life and go into treatment, whereas a lot of people function with eating disorders for a very long time because it hasn't hijacked their existence. That's what I come across a lot – people saying, 'Yeah, I get sick three times a week or at weekends if I overeat,' and that's harder to kick. It's like casual smoking – it's easier to give up something you do all the time than something you do casually.

T: Would you like to be able to talk about the bulimia on stage in stand-up?

JM: I don't think it would work, no. Me and PJ are both adopted, so we wrote a show called *Separated at Birth* about our adoptions and we toured that for a while. In it, I had one or two 'jokes' about being in treatment for an eating disorder, and it just didn't work because the audience are kind of like, 'What?' and then you're back into something else. Some things need a longer stage time.

T: Did you go looking for your [birth] parents?

JM: Yeah.

T: Were they together? Were they in Ireland?

JM: One of them was, one of them was in Australia. I'd always been really curious. My brother Connor never cared but I really latched on to it. I was trying to decide whether or not to do it, and then when I met PJ it was really nice because I'd never really spent a huge amount of time with anyone who was adopted before so I'd never heard anyone's story. He tipped me over the edge to try and track them down. It was amazing, it's mental, it's mental.

T: Can you tell us what happened?

JM: I contacted the agency that I'd been adopted from and they contacted my biological mother and she got in touch straight away. As an adopted person, you don't look like anyone in your family and I always wanted to look like someone. I was always really jealous of people who looked like their siblings. You feel alone, you've nothing to mirror.

T: And are your parents African or something?!

JM: They might as well be!

T: Do you definitely not look like your adopted parents?

JM: Nothing like them! Even the way I loved performing and wanted to go to the Billie Barry [Stage School], and there was none of that!

T: So at what age did you cop on: *'You guys are no craic, you can't be my parents!'*?

JM: They can't even tap-dance! *What is this?* I always thought that Twink was my mother. This is as a child. And Johnny Logan! I used to watch the Eurovision. I thought I could sing, so I was like Twink and Johnny Logan, that'd be what I'd go for [if I could choose biological parents]! If Twink wasn't available, I'd take Linda Martin. Anyway, I sent off the letter. My biological mother – we'll call her 'Claire' – Claire wrote back, and in it she put a picture of herself. And I was like, *'No, no, that's not right. It's not right. No!'* She looked the image of my adoptive mother. They're so alike. To the point where I went online – and I had her first name and her second name now (you get that when she agrees to have contact with you) – and found a woman . . . I swear to God when I say she *was* the image of me – this woman up in Donegal, this absolute randomer, who was an artist, a poet – it was uncanny.

So I contacted *her*. There was a gin taken! She had this Facebook profile about her business and it said she'd emigrated in 1983 from Donegal – and I was born in 1983. So I was like, 'That can't be a coincidence.' We have the same hairstyle. She emigrated in 1983. So I contacted her and I was like, 'Basically, you're not going to believe this but, I'm home!' I was like, 'Are you my biological mother?' And she wrote back really fast, which was very kind of her and she said, 'No, I'm not.' And I didn't believe her.

I lost it. I'd built it up in my mind, I'd so much expectation around it. I didn't believe her because you hear about women who give their kids up for adoption and the kids will come to look for them and they'll deny it ever happened because they haven't told their husband or they haven't told their kids and they don't want to bring all that up. So I figured that's why . . . so, I wrote back *again* and this time I took loads of pictures from her Facebook page and pictures from my Facebook page and put them side by side, like in a collage, to kind of go, 'Who are you kidding here?'

And then she shut down her Facebook page.

T: Yeah, it is the start of a kind of crazy-bitch-serial-killer movie!

JM: It is. She was right to shut down her Facebook page because I wouldn't have stopped! But I did an interview, me and PJ must have been promoting *Separated at Birth*, and she contacted me and said, 'I just heard you on a radio show and you said you'd met your biological mother and I'm delighted for you,' so that was nice. No restraining order or anything, it all worked out grand.

T: Fair play to you . . . so, your dad went to Australia?

JM: So I got his name off my biological mother, straight into Facebook, found him straight away, and I'm the image of him. *Image of him*. Which was amazing. And he has loads of sons and they're all me if I was a boy, which was great. So I emailed him on Facebook and he never wrote back to me. And so I was like, right, let's just park that, he's obviously a wanker. Then about a year passed and one morning I got a random email from him saying my email had gone into his junk folder and his sixteen-year-old son had found it and read it out to him. I must have written the letter having watched an episode of *Dallas*, because it was really dramatic – 'I hope you're sitting down, I'm your daughter!' Can you imagine his son reading this out, saying, 'Dad, what were you up to thirty-three years ago?!'

T: So were you a secret?

JM: Well, his kids didn't know, but his wife knew. And he's really nice. We email pretty regularly and we're going to meet soon. He's like, 'I consider you completely one of my kids.'

T: It seems like you've had a life of great drama – self-inflicted and projected!

JM: That's a great way of explaining it, actually.

T: And is part of your interest in stand-up that when you're onstage, nobody tells you what you're going to talk about or the way in which you're going to talk about it? You have a voice and you can treat your experiences with humour. Is that part of the power of it?

JM: That's what it's becoming. In the beginning, I was doing it because I was being encouraged to do it and I knew it was something I was kind of good at. Being onstage is what makes me happy. I like taking the piss out of things. I know that when I was promoting *Bite Me*, some people were giving me stick, saying I was mocking eating disorders, but I was doing the opposite. I'm telling you my story and hoping you laugh with me at the funny bits. It's an irreverent look at eating disorders, it's not mocking it. Anyway, they say comedy is tragedy multiplied by time. My time is like thirty seconds.

Joe Brolly

'You've got to throw in the odd hand grenade:
it just brightens everything.'

Tommy: I was drinking with you in Belfast not so long ago and I left annoyed at you.

Joe Brolly: I know.

T: I felt like you were trying to wind me up the whole time.

JB: I thought what I said to you was a compliment! That what I've always found about you is that you're more interesting than funny. I thought that was a compliment. And you said, 'Ya fucking prick!' He said this thing – it was very funny and I went into hysterics – he said that on a Friday night, he loves talking about breasts and stuff like that, which I do too, but not on telly. He said that when his wife lowered her breasts down on his face on a Friday night, he said it was like absolution, forgiving all your sins.

T: It's like being forgiven.

JB: I thought it was brilliant!

T: She's at home now, mortified.

JB: I'd have thought she's gone past that at this stage. That's true, you know, I think a moment like that does reprogramme you, because we get overcome with natural emotion. In Holland now, for manic depression, what they're doing is resetting people's brains by – obviously, it's a medicinal dosage – two doses of MDMA two weeks apart to flood their brain with endorphins and to give them that sort of fresh start. So I thought what you said there was very profound.

T: Well, they used to do that in America. Ecstasy was a tablet they took for marital reconnection or something like that. It was over the counter and legal.

You're a fantastic writer and I love reading your stuff. I read an article that you wrote recently about RTÉ and I found it very inspiring because you hit the nail on the head in terms of what RTÉ does to creative people. I wonder would you share some of that with me again? The impression I got from it was that you had a feeling that it was almost dangerous to be creative here.

JB: It is, and I felt that when I came into *The Sunday Game*, which I loved. I loved every minute of it. To be asked. And then to be palling about with the greats of football and then to have the red carpet into Croke Park on a Sunday and to be part of the national conversation. I loved it. We were free to express our opinions. I felt that I could talk about football – actually talk about it. So the way the lads in the pub talk about it. Like, no one in the pub says, 'Kerry had a 25.7 per cent productivity rating in the first five minutes but in fact that increased to 31.2 per cent in the second quarter of the first half . . .' You'd be taken away by the men in the white coats.

T: Yeah.

JB: We're talking about football – this is our fun, our recreation, what we love – you love it and you hate it. Of course, it's personal when you're talking about the GAA, because people take it very personally. It's a very deep and spiritual connection with the game, which I love very passionately.

So, it started to become statistics-driven, and then we started to get sent scripts. Before the All-Ireland Football

Final this year a script was sent out. 'You'll say this and then he'll deal with this and you'll deal with that.' And you know the way you pick out a package of [clips for] analysis, which I always loved doing. Then we were told what to pick out. And I rang and I said, 'You don't need me, you need a news-reader. You need a narrator.' Eventually the ground just shrank under me.

And then: the All-Ireland Final – which I thought was great fun, the draw. We had a brilliant day and there was some controversy during the game – the referee, who's a good pal of mine, gave a decision and I had a bit of a blast at it. It was good fun, and you can sense that too. I sense a very strong connection with the audience. I went on the Dublin side for it. And it was great – 'cause you've got to throw in the odd hand grenade: it just brightens everything. And I can imagine people on their sofas, some clapping and enjoying it, some ready to tear their hair out. It was great fun.

And then I got a series of warnings after that game. For example, I was told, 'It's outrageous. Your position in RTÉ is probably untenable now because at eleven minutes past three you said to Pat Spillane, "Would you stop patting my arm?"' I said, 'Have you lost your fucking mad marbles?' Me and Pat are like an auld married couple and that's part of the fun of it!

When I grabbed his arm at the end of the game, I warmly congratulated him about his nephew Killian [Spillane], who had been magnificent when he came on. There's always been that family thing with us, but that's gone now. People are being brought in and prepared to just recite statistics and stuff. It's an awful pity, because it's not real.

T: The most attractive thing for me watching *The Sunday Game* – and I know I'm not just speaking for myself – is watching yourself, Colm, and Pat, and marvellously hosted by Michael, going at it. And I am stunned that there isn't an eye on protecting that and encouraging it. You're going to be missed.

JB: Well, look, I was there for twenty years and, genuinely, I loved it. The fun that we had. That public conversation that we had was great. I could go into a bar in Belmullet or Manorhamilton or Cahersiveen and immediately the fun starts, the roar goes up, everybody talks. Also, the other thing that I was very privileged with, and still am, is that people confess to me and they also know that I write a column, so they'd say, 'I'll tell you a good one.' All of that for me was very precious, and then for it to end so abruptly like that, and I thought cruelly, I have to say . . . I'm a big boy, but I have to say I was shocked.

T: I was shocked as well. Tell me, does the flak not knock a strip off you at all? People giving out about you, etcetera?

JB: It's not real because it's GAA people – we all know each other and we know that there are limits. It's like the panto. In the GAA community, we've still got that sense of solidarity and unity, and if they're doing well in Meath or Cork, then we're doing well in Derry. That sense of brotherhood. You can travel anywhere in the world to a GAA place and you'll be immediately helped and embraced.

T: And do you still coach in Belfast?

JB: Yeah, I coach the minors. This is my third year with them now, and it was the U16s for three years before that. If somebody said to me, you can get £10 million this year or you can coach the minors, I would stay on the minors, definitely. We've had so much fun over the years, we're always experimenting, and we play adventurous football.

One time – and this comes into my mind now because I

was clearing out some stuff the other day and I saw it in a cardboard box in the downstairs loo – I was working with the boys on scoring goals. What everybody does to score a goal, until they're taught it, is they'll run as hard as they can in the alleyway that's free and then they'll kick across to the goals. And every keeper will take a step out and then dive to the middle. The keeper will save it if I kick it at him. Anyway, I had this idea in my mind that the keeper is a figure of fun. I always loved the great [Meath inter-county footballer] Bernie Flynn, and so we have a dummy that we do in training that we call 'the Bernie Flynn', which I showed the boys. (Actually, we met Bernie – me and a lot of the minors one day outside Croke Park – and I said, 'This is Bernie Flynn,' and they went mental.)

And then I hit on this idea. They were about fourteen at a time so I had to be careful and say nothing to the parents; I got this blow-up doll – it was a nurse! Once the parents were away, you put it in the centre of the goals, you see. It just sort of wobbled about a bit. We put the boys on this side and on that side and we did the various dummies. So we were doing this and they were laughing their heads off, and very quickly that translated into, 'We'll put a real keeper in there now.' You wouldn't see that in a coach's manual. At the start they were kicking it at the blow-up doll and the team mates were laughing – but eventually they got used to it. You're passing it into the net, you're not driving it across. You get your angles right.

T: Tell us, the law in Belfast. You work as a barrister, defending and prosecuting?

JB: No, just defending. You're dealing with poverty. That's what crime is. Crime just comes from poverty, apart from the most serious crimes, like white-collar crimes – the billions being moved around that cause most of the problems, the tax evasion, all those sorts of things that cause your homelessness and your food banks. But the people who suffer most from the criminal law are people that suffer most from inequality. So in my job, it's the underdog all the time. People who may have lost both parents as children, maybe a father murdered a mother. In the last six to eight months I've had clients who have died from drug overdose or been murdered. Just last week I was at a funeral of a young lad only twenty-four years of age whose brother was murdered in April and his parents have now lost both their sons.

I was representing a man a few years ago who before his trial started he came up and hugged me. He was a man who had been an engineer and he was quoting Seamus Heaney, tears coming down his face and all cuts on his face. The trial was due to start the next day and he had come to see me and we had some tea together, and the next morning he died on the street. We lit some candles on the street three days later, and that's the reality, you know? It's poverty. Drugs come from poverty, as you know, because you don't have a better alternative.

I took in a homeless kid for about nine months or so, and about three weeks later we went to a funeral of his best friend who had died of hypothermia. If you're on the streets, you're hopeless. It's a huge problem all over the world, and in Ireland now, which needs to be dealt with systemically. But that's what attracted me to it.

T: That's what attracted you to it?

JB: Yeah. I have an appetite for the underdog, which I suppose is why I got involved. I was going to tell you this story about the kid who came to me. He was homeless and he had started taking heroin, because it's a very, very long day, it's freezing, and you don't know where your next bite is coming from. You might get into a hostel, but hostels can be unpredictable and sometimes violent. But heroin mostly starts in the homeless community and then it spreads out. They give them heroin to start with to get them hooked and then that leads to petty crime. You burgle houses and shops and you become desperate. So he came to live with me and, basically, I just let him do what he was doing and we just treated him with love and respect.

T: Who was in the family home at the time?

JB: It was just me in mine. All my kids and all. We just live around the corner and they got to know him very well and embraced him, put up the Christmas decorations together. We have a very amicable situation – I wouldn't be the easiest man to live with. Once he was nourished and looking better and stronger, he started going to job interviews and we saw the zero-hours economy and how evil that was. He got a call about a job in McDonald's and he was so excited. He wore one of my suits to the interview, but the suit was far too big on him! He went to McDonald's and he got the job, and he was absolutely delighted. Then he got a phone call the night before saying, 'You're needed for two hours in the morning.' Then he would get a phone call saying, 'You need to be here at eleven o'clock' – sure he had no way of getting there that time so he lost the job. He had no protections. Anyway, now he's in his own flat, he's working on a site, doing terribly well, playing Gaelic football. I'm going to go up and do a coaching session with him now in the New Year. But it was a classic example – all he needed was a hand-out, a bit of stability, accommodation, not having to pay bills.

T: But Joe, it's one thing to notice that and it's another thing to provide it.

JB: It's basic enough stuff. A big moment for me was giving away my kidney.

T: You gave your kidney? To who?

JB: Just a fella, he was a stranger then. I had a superficial view of the world at that point; I had won an All-Ireland, I was very successful in court – newspaper column, television, people talking about you all the time. It was superficial, really.

T: The court stuff doesn't sound superficial.

JB: No, but the way that I took the kudos from that was sustained by all that other nonsense. The kidney donation brought me deeper into life – real life – and I began to see the reality for other people. That, for me, is the big thing with inequality. What's the point in having a lot of people around if you don't have anything? There's no fun in that, and the reality is that equality is good for everyone.

I think that, in politics, the conversation needs to be changed. So, if you criticize J. P. Morgan's CEO, or if you criticize Dell's CEO, because he's got a gigantic yacht with a full-sized basketball court on it and a man coming behind with a boat on the minimum wage who picks up the basketballs, if you criticize him, you're a communist and a socialist. *'These are the guys providing employment.'* The conversation needs to change. Equality is good for everyone. Society needs minor adjustments.

What's the point in owning an island in the Caribbean and going on a private jet if nurses are queuing up at food banks and we can't sufficiently pay our teachers so that the best people are going elsewhere and doing other things. What's happening now is the private money markets, the financial markets, they're hoovering up all our brightest and best kids. Our kids are going through the education factory, get to the age of eighteen, and they're good at exams and they're very commercialized now. The new generation are dangerously commercialized now. They go into financial institutions, the big gambling companies, and then they spend their precious years working out how best to exploit their fellow man.

And now we're seeing society starting to come apart slowly but surely all over the world. We see it in America, the dangerous rise of the far right, the demagogue, the fake news stuff where nothing is real. It all stems from inequality. The ironic thing about inequality is how the powerful manipulate it to keep themselves where they are. The poorest people are the ones who suffer, yet they in many circumstances are the ones who support the system.

T: Is the work in the court relentless?

JB: Well, no, it's not, because I'm freelance so I'm not accountable to anyone. We had a very dramatic trial about three weeks ago in the courts. I have to say I still love the drama of it – 'Are you ready to proceed, Mr Brolly?'! The first witness, I left him for about thirty seconds, pretending I was looking through papers, you know . . . This is a thing that people say about me, compared to outside of court, where I'm very approachable and talk a lot of sense and all, in court I'm absolutely relentless and overwhelming. I enjoy the whole court discipline, and I'm allowed to do it in court because the rule is simple; I defend the client to the best of my ability within the law. The secret of courtroom advocacy is persuasion, and to persuade you need to be a choreographer, so that in the end no one can think of any alternative to what it is you're proposing.

T: . . . To 'Brolly world'!

JB: Well, exactly! It's a psychological . . .

T: . . . Torture!

JB: Well, no. The thing about my game is that because

you're immersed in it you reach a stage when the courtroom door opens and the witness comes up, and you're thinking, unless they're a really good con-man or con-woman, you've got them. People can't conceal who they are. You clock them then. Some witnesses may think this is very dangerous, I'll stay away from the evidence, stay around the sides, I'll leave them completely unsatisfied and leave the jury slightly confused.

It is a very interesting discipline. I believe that it's all a farce anyway, that this is just keeping the people from the ghettos under control. That's really what it is in the end. I don't have any compunction about –

T: Doing whatever you have to do?

JB: Yeah, because it's a charade. 'Tough on crime, tough on the causes of crime.' If you want to be tough on crime, build council houses. In 1977 in England, they were building a hundred thousand council houses a year. Last year, they built six thousand. Of course there's going to be homelessness and poverty. Dublin's become obscene – people are advertising deluxe garden sheds to rent. We have beautiful country in the West entirely being neglected. Why don't we move civil servants and university campuses out to the West, and start building council houses there? I mean, how dear would it be to build a high-speed rail system that joins up the West? Knock Airport should be an international hub. These places are magnificent places to live, with a great quality of life. Those communities are being systematically destroyed.

JB: Wasn't it you who bought the big Robert de Niro-style Winnebago? And then you couldn't . . .

T: I couldn't get it up the road.

JB: Tell us that story.

T: Well, when you spend your life on the road, you're always trying to reinvent it. The truth of it is you can never get over driving the miles, but you always think, if only I had a helicopter. it'd make it easier! So I thought to myself, I'm staying in all these hotels so I'll buy myself a proper RV and live in it. I'll do the show and then I'll drive out by a river and sleep in that. So I bought this thing – I swear to you, I just pressed 'pay in euro' on the website, I didn't even see it. About three weeks later, a thing about the size of the *QE2* pulled in outside of the house. The guy that drove it over from Germany, he didn't speak much English so he came into the house and fell asleep on the couch for twelve hours – that's how stressful the drive had been for him!

Then I had a gig to do in Enniskillen. The road to Sligo isn't too bad, but Sligo across to Enniskillen is a small road. My tour manager was driving, but it was a left-hand drive with the seat slightly to the left of the wheel. Trucks kept coming towards us and you'd see the drivers going, *'Pull in! Pull in!'* I went to sleep on the couch because I couldn't deal with the stress of it. A wing mirror got taken off, and we said we'd never drive this fuckin' thing again!

Then I was doing a charity gig – Gay Byrne used to do this fundraiser for orphans in Belarus – and at the end of the gig I said, 'I've been so moved by the plight of these children with no parents that I'm going to give them my motorhome!' We were told that they wouldn't accept it because you can't just drive into Russia, you'd be stuck too long at the border and there'd be too many papers to fill in. So, it was out in the shed for a long time and the funny sad ending to this story is that a friend of mine, the bank repossessed his house and evicted him, and he's living in it now.

JB: Brilliant.

T: That's how these things turn around. Are you going to be talking at all during the summer about football? Do you have any platform now?

JB: Well, I still write in the *Sunday Independent*.

T: Yourself and Colm O'Rourke and a couple of other sports journalists are the reason I buy the *Sunday Independent*, because I think your writing is that good.

JB: It's a bit like this show, or a lot of chat shows – what people actually want, particularly the younger generation, is edgy, controversial people speaking their minds. I remember Gay Byrne taking a condom – I had never seen a condom, and whenever I came to Trinity, condoms were banned unless you got them on prescription. I remember the guards came into the students' union and confiscated the condom machine. It was a girl from Belfast who was the student welfare and they carried it down the stairs like a coffin over their shoulder. We were shouting, 'Oh, you black bastards!' (that's what we said to the RUC) – I remember when he [Gay Byrne] took the condom out, and he said, 'Let's see what all of the fuss is about.' I mean, the country was spellbound. You know, he did that, and it was a regular thing with him and he did it without fear.

T: We have to wind this up now, but is the only place that you'll be talking about the football this summer in the column? And maybe on a podcast?

JB: And the pub.

T: And the pub. I wish you were on the telly, Joe.

John Connors

'The reality is that because we were nomadic,
we assimilated less than the rest of settled Irish culture
and were able to actually hold on to a lot more of
Irish culture, and we're being persecuted for that.'

Tommy: *'I'm a travelling man, singing my song for you . . .'*

John Connors: It's a good thing you know me!

T: Initially when I heard John Connors, I thought, the fella that trains McGregor? No, of course I know you. I had the pleasure of hearing you sing in the National Concert Hall.

JC: That was a great night – well, it was actually a shit night until Liam Ó Maonlaí blew the roof off the place. I said, 'God help the man that follows him,' and then it was you and you were absolutely brilliant.

T: You're very kind.

JC: I'm not slagging you now.

T: Well, if you are, I didn't notice! I have a fierce grá for the travelling people, genuinely I do. I kind of know in my heart and soul that part of me wishes I was a traveller.

JC: You do a good impression of a traveller!

T: I do a lot of material about travellers, as you know . . .

JC: I know, I seen you for years, sure.

T: . . . And I've crossed the line a few times, but that's what the line is there for.

JC: But I'm a big comedy fan and I think there's very few bounds for comedy anyway, you should be allowed to go where you want as long as it's not malicious and there's a point behind it.

T: I was doing a show in Lucan recently and I started talking about the travelling people and the part envy, part fear I have for them, and this group of lads started cheering in the room and we started this dialogue.

I was saying, 'I love yous, lads.

And they said, 'We love you, Thomas Tiernan, we love you so much.'

I said to them that because I was spending a lot of time driving around the country and passing by so many halting sites, I would love to be able to swing in for a cup of tea. I would just love to be able to pull the big 7 series BMW in! I would genuinely love that, but I always have a fear about how you would be taken, would the dogs ate you, would I recognize some of me washing on the clothesline . . . But I would love to do that.

So I was asking the lads in the gig – and I mean this, John, I have a huge heart for ye – I said to the lads, 'Now that we're getting on so well, do I have permission to walk on to any halting site in the country and I'd be given a cup of tea?', and this is what they said to me: 'Anywhere you want, Tom, anywhere you want – except Ballinasloe!'

JC: That's the thing, and it's an interesting point, that travellers are very regional people and very clannish among their own people. I did an article recently with the *Journal* and I was making some point about mental health and the suicide rate among travellers, and a fella commented underneath saying, 'Well, that's all well and good, but what about my dog, he was robbed down in Ballinasloe the other day around the corner from my house.' And I'm saying, 'What the ... I haven't a clue about your dog, I don't know who them travellers are.' So that's the thing – we all do get bunched into the one big community, but we're all actually a very diverse community all across the country. But if you want to come to any site, come to mine. Genuinely, come over for a cup of tea and have a chat, meet my grandmother.

T: No!

JC: Well, go fuck yourself!

T: She's probably only about thirty-seven! So how many travellers are in the country?

JC: The census will tell you about thirty thousand, and around fifteen hundred up North, but I think there's a lot more than that.

T: And in England then as well?

JC: Yeah, ten or fifteen thousand. There's a lot more gypsies in England.

T: And in terms of making a living, my kids go to school with traveller kids and the traveller kids tend to leave before or after the Junior Cert or something like that, and so what do they go doing?

JC: Well, the tradition was obviously tinsmen, but then that went out the window with plastic and all that. In the later years now, it's been anything with your hands, anything you can graft at, any sort of job like that. But there is a change in the last ten years because before that it would be rare to get a traveller to even enter secondary school and now they're doing Junior and Leaving Cert, and that's a very good thing, but it can be a negative thing as well. You're probably thinking how can it be negative, but when a lot of travellers get into the education system, they feel like they have to conform, change their accent, and kind of be somebody else to get on easier, and that's not good because you're living behind your culture and who you are. A big part of [being a traveller] is our identity and how proud we are of where we come from, so there is a lot of that pressure when you go to higher-level education.

T: I can actually speak a bit of cant.

JC: Can you?

T: [*speaks cant*] That means . . .

JC: Don't be saying what it means, that's our language! Are you looking for a fight?

T: No, I'm not looking for a fight, a dance maybe! Do travellers still travel?

JC: No, they don't.

T: Wasn't that half the craic of being a traveller?

JC: No, actually, that's actually the misconception. Travelling has just been a vehicle to protect our culture. Most people don't even realize that in Gaelic Ireland, for the most part, a majority of the people on the island were nomadic. We were probably the most nomadic country in the world and were still majority nomadic until around the 1500s and the reconquest of Ireland. And if you look at the things that have been attacked in our culture, like our family system, the way we set up on sites, that clan culture and nomadism was a way of protecting our culture. But we can't travel any more because it's against the law. We'd love to be still travelling, but it's impossible now.

T: How is it impossible to travel?

JC: Well, there's various different laws and regulations and policies that were brought in so you can't camp in council land or other land. There's a number of old traveller camps in the thirty-two counties which were the ones you'd keep going back to, and every single one of them was blocked over by boulders. Any place you see with a field and boulders, that was a former traveller camp – they actually got that from the councils in England after they went over to see how they dealt with travellers and gypsies. They came back here and they brought the boulder technique, and that's how they stopped all the campsites.

T: It does seem that if you weren't tied to a house, one of the glories of having wheels under your bedroom would be to travel.

JC: The thing is, the word 'traveller' doesn't do us justice at all as a culture of people. We're not travellers anywhere, we're *Mincéir*, that's what our language is and there's no translation for that other than that's who we are. And I don't want there to be a translation for that. 'Traveller' doesn't really fit into who we are, that's only an aspect of it.

T: It's quite a nice word though, in fairness.

JC: Well, it's a lot better than 'knacker' or 'pikey' or anything like that.

T: I would know a lot of people from Tuam, and the Tuam word for a traveller would be 'the Minks' and that's coming from *Mincéir*, is it?

JC: I don't know because I'm from a different region, but I'd say that's where it's coming from. That's not offensive, and even the word 'tinker' wasn't an offensive word. My grandfather and grandmother would call themselves tinkers, not travellers, but what happened was it ended up as a derogatory word because settled people would call other settled people it as they thought it was a bad thing and then it became a bad name. But I wouldn't take offence to 'tinker'.

T: Tell me about arranged marriages, how does that all work? Is every marriage arranged?

JC: No, not at all, very few nowadays are arranged. I actually wouldn't have a problem with arranged marriage – that goes back to Gaelic Ireland. The cousin marriage thing, which I'm not exactly for, is also less common now, that was a Gaelic Irish thing too. If you were in a *túath*, you couldn't marry outside your third cousin unless you were the head of a clan. All the weddings were arranged and there were always young marriages back in Gaelic Ireland. At twelve and thirteen, they were getting married, and it may be seen as negative to some people but really that's the remains of Gaelic Ireland that the travellers are keeping going. A lot has changed. Even social media has changed for travellers in terms of marriage because you're meeting travellers from different sides of the country instead of just your own region. It could be within Leinster between two or three different counties, or a Donegal traveller can meet a Cork traveller online. The arranged marriages are really only done in a few families now, really, and you'd still be asked do you want to. It's not like you have to, but they'd want it because it was a part of the culture.

T: The traveller girls that I know from around Galway, they're beautiful-looking, gorgeous women, but they do seem to be a bit more . . . I remember asking someone about them and they said, 'You'll never see her walking around on her own, there'll always be someone with her.' So is that part of putting manners on them or controlling them or something?

JC: Well, there's a thing in our culture called 'scandal', so they have to go in groups. It's just the way it is, they go in groups so someone couldn't say that you'd done this or that. And they want to go in groups, and even traveller men do the same, even me and my cousins. I could be going to the garage for a bottle of Coke and I'd say it to my cousins, 'Do you want to go over?' We'd go over in a herd and we get

The state has always wanted to assimilate us and make us a settled people, and that was the official policy. Traveller children were literally taken from their families and put into homes – one less in the itinerant class. A lot of people don't even know this kind of thing now.

There's criminal elements in our community, there's no doubt about that, but look at racism. I did another documentary recently, a two-part series about Native Americans and African Americans, and it was really interesting because I looked at racism over there. Racism is very different everywhere you go because there's different histories, obviously, but there's the same results from racism, state racism, institutionalized racism: high incarceration, high crime, low education, high unemployment. The problem in Ireland is even the liberals will attack travellers, because travellers have been completely dehumanized.

A part of the narrative has been the whole famine myth that we came from the Famine, which has been disproved for years, but no one ever wanted to know about it. And in terms of the agenda of re-assimilating travellers like they were 'failed settled people', if they were never acknowledging that we were our own people, then you might ask, 'Why did they want to re-assimilate us anyway? What was the problem?' Well, when the Free State government was formed, they were trying to create a new Ireland and they wanted big foreign investment, especially from America. There was many politicals talking about the ugly image of the tinker that would shoo away foreign investment. Even in the early 20s you got newspaper clippings of travellers painted as beasts drinking and whatever, the exact same propaganda pictures that were used seventy or eighty years previously in

New York and London about the Irish. Everything that has been attached to us Irish as a whole has been put on to travellers – thieves, clannish, prudish, dumb, everything.

The reality is that because we were nomadic, we assimilated less than the rest of settled Irish culture and were able to actually hold on to a lot more of Irish culture, and we're being persecuted for that. There's a lot of criminal elements in the whole of our community, a lot of it, but you have to look at the whole picture and the whole context.

T: Mixed education would seem to me to be the key. Parents might be racist or have hatred towards travellers or immigrants or stuff like that, but when your kids are in the same school together, it's much easier for them to have ordinary, wonderful, good-craic relationships with everybody.

JC: It is. I want to see the documentary we did shown in schools, and I want to see traveller week every year in schools because I was never taught anything about my history. One day, one of my teachers said to me, 'You came from the Famine,' and that was that. That's the only education I got, and in schools I was segregated and put in a different class until my mother was so angry because I was reading books that I had been reading three years previously and just drawing with crayons. My mother had to go and give out to the teachers before I could go back into my normal classes. And it's still going on in the country right now, with traveller children still being segregated, so there's a huge problem with the educational system. A lot of travellers in, say, 6th class, who are eleven or twelve, should be able to read or write in some form, but some of them can't at all because they're just given crayons or books they were given in junior infants.

T: Is it more difficult to be a traveller on this island than it is to be a settled person?

JC: That's the best joke you've had all night! It's hard being anybody on this island right now . . . But of course it is, 100 per cent. There's been studies done about racism in Ireland with sixth-year students, young people who would be the most liberal and progressive. They were asked who wouldn't mind having a person of colour next door as a neighbour, and 97 per cent said they wouldn't mind. When they were asked how many of you wouldn't mind having a traveller as a next-door neighbour, 95 per cent said they *would* mind, so that will give you the margin of racism. And that's every single day. I went down to Tuam, where there was a traveller who was the mayor of Tuam. Yet I went down there doing a little documentary, talking to all these young travellers, and there were literally streets that they can't walk down. They're not allowed in any shop, any restaurant, any hotel, anywhere. They just completely accept it, which is what angered me.

T: It's probably one of those things where, say with a traveller wedding or something like that, chaos can occur that then infects the conversation.

JC: Well, it creates fear. I remember I was down at a nightclub just around the corner from my place and every single night there were vicious arguments outside, people glassing each other, every night. It was settled people, not travellers. I went there and never caused any trouble, but when a traveller breaks up a place or whatever, it creates more fear, and the fear is what's driving everything. If we meet each other and there's a fear of each other, or a settled person being awkward because they're afraid, well, then the traveller could react like, 'Fuck them.'

I remember going to a pub one time a few years ago to watch a match with a cousin of mine. There was no one in the pub, and then a bunch of five or six other travellers came in. We didn't really know them, but we sat down with them, and the way it is with travellers is we kind of know each other and we'll have a drink. We had great craic, and then the manager walked over and said, 'Lads, you're going to have to leave.' It was six o'clock on a Sunday and the match was at six thirty. When we asked why, he said, 'Ah, lads, you're getting a bit loud, but it's not really me, it's the owner, who's back there.' And I said, 'We're only having a laugh, I'm not leaving.' So they rang the guards, and they said we had to go.

People have been conditioned this way. If you're a settled person and you've never had an experience of a traveller and you're reading that they're this and that and the other, you've been conditioned to think like that. What I'm trying to do is to decondition those people, and decondition travellers as well from their negative attitudes towards settled people too.

T: I was going to ask you, what are the worst habits of the settled people in the eyes of the travelling people?

JC: They're margarine-eaters.

T: They're what?

JC: They're margarine-eaters! 'See them margarine-eating bastards!' That was our slag. I remember my mother brought us to the chipper and we were out in this park, sitting down eating whatever it was, and these couple of settled fellows came along, and they were a few years older than me and they were saying, 'You knackers,' and honestly, at this point you wouldn't even care, and me and my brother Joe jumped up and said, 'You margarine-eating bastards.' So it ended up being a good little thing to numb the whole thing. Yeah, that and maybe that settled women would be a bit more ... 'chancey' than traveller women.

T: So there's positive side effects!

JC: There's a saying among travellers – 'Never trust a settled person, because all you'll ever be is a knacker,' and that runs very deep, just like it runs with settled people the other way. It is hard to deconstruct that. My best friend in the world is a settled fella, but I know travellers would see him and say, 'You'd never really trust them, though.' Years ago, I would have said, 'Yeah, totally,' but now I can trust them 100 per cent, because he's my friend. It doesn't matter where he's from or if he's a traveller or a settled person, and so we have to get over that as well ourselves.

Jon Kenny

'When the wildness goes you kind of know it's time to hang up the boots. You must always feel as if you never want to lose that kind of madness, like the young giddy heifer on the way to the fair, like, tail cocked in the air...'

Tommy: How are you?

Jon Kenny: I'm getting old, but we're all right. We're good, actually. We're good.

T: You're on the road with Mary [McEvoy] for *The Matchmaker*?

JK: Yeah, myself and Mary would be touring, tramping around the area. On and off, you know. We're doing a few shows, and I have another show as well, *Crowman*. That's a new play. It's good, it's dark, very dark bit of humour in it.

T: What's it about?

JK: It's about a guy who lives on his own. He's a bit strange, which I can relate to, like. He's a bit of a loner. It's a beautiful story, actually. He becomes isolated by his life for different reasons and we join him in his late fifties. And if something happens, he hears a bit of news, all of a sudden it starts a kind of a chain reaction about stuff that he's gone through in his life. He hears that a friend of his has passed away so it kind of takes off from there, but it's very clever, a lot of pathos here and there, a bit of madness. It's set in the present time and about how easy it is for anyone to end up on their own surrounded with everything, mobile phones and internet and everything, but really, they're no good to him because this guy is actually just on his own. The character is living in rural Ireland, and it's just the whole idea of how easy it is to become isolated away from your community. The community that he lives in, the 'nowhere' that he spends time with, is not the community that surrounds him. He's become disconnected from that a little bit for different reasons.

T: Is it violent?

JK: It touches on it, yeah, because it's stuff that's happened in his life. Probably towards him too. He doesn't go into any great graphic detail in it, but there is an anger in it in a sense and an anger that was probably perpetrated towards him at different stages in his life from simple things, like the idea that he might be bullied growing up or something. The fact that the old man and himself didn't get on and maybe the old man preferred the brother.

T: Where does the crow thing come into it?

JK: He's a man who loves nature, but the crows have triggered something in him, and there's a reason for that as well. So it's dark, it's mad, it's funny. It was written by a young writer from Charleville called Katie Holly and it's her third play. People have said to me, like, 'How did a young female write this?' Because it's really on the pulse of something that most people think is a very male domain, and yet she hits it right on the head.

T: Is it set in and around north Cork?

JK: It is, kind of close to where I'm from, so the dialect and the language is stuff you'd hear nowadays talking to people and they don't speak good English. It's a mix of all the stuff that's happening, so it's right up to date, but it's still stuck on the Cork–Limerick border with lads using language that their grandfathers used maybe, which is lovely. I hope we never lose it.

T: Do you feel like you're giving due respect? Like this is an opportunity to pay homage to men from your part of the country that went that way, that ended up *aisteach*, as they say.

JK: Not just for my part of the country. I think it's beautiful because it just shows his sensitivity, that behind this man, his weaknesses, his vulnerability, he has strength as well to keep going. And then it's beautiful because no matter what he's been through, he says, 'Tomorrow is another day, life isn't that bad.' There's that bit of redemption and all of a sudden even the audience go, 'Thanks be to God.'

T: I often wonder about being free from comedy. Having spent so long working that and working the comic angle – and I look at your stuff an awful lot on YouTube and it still makes me laugh – but I'm wondering is it a relief to be onstage and just angry?

JK: Feckin' Jesus, I was always feckin' angry! There's anger in comedy, and sure you know yourself – comedy, Jesus, it's nothing but frustration, really, in a funny way. But yeah, it's nice to kind of get away. And it's nearly five or six years now since I've actually done a stand-up gig, which is like withdrawal from it. I just wanted to stop doing it because I was finding I didn't want to be funny any more, and it's not that I don't enjoy being funny, I love going out and having the craic – Jesus: stop! – but it was just the whole idea of 'let's try and do something different or let's just experience different things,' and maybe let an audience experience something different. I love doing what I do because I love John B. Keane, I love his language – real earthiness, real richness. It's a mix – there's bits of pagan in it, there's bits of Irish in it, there's bits of everything in it. And it's great fun to do that, and there's great characters and stuff.

T: And that John B. stuff is violent *and* funny.

JK: Well, it is, absolutely, it's dreadful, it's savage. I mean, when you think of *Sive*, it's like child slavery, it's just bartering with human life for land, for money. But it's very hard to think that we're only a step away from all that, it's not back in ancient times, it was maybe in the 30s or 40s of the last century.

T: And it's happening now to women who aren't Irish, young women from Eastern Europe and parts of Asia, Africa, South America, that bartering of young women to auld lads with the horn . . . I mean, that's not the way it was phrased in the United Nations . . .

JK: Not exactly. But even talking like that about Keane, everyone thinks *The Matchmaker* is kind of traditional – the thing is full of sex. That's all 'tis about. Sex and riding is all they wanted. And he disguised it beautifully. *Sive* is like that as well. There's humour in it, but at the same time it is quite tragic and it's quite savage.

But getting back to your point about getting away from comedy, yeah, a break is good. I did a charity gig about two months ago. There was a lot of bands on at the gig and so a few lads asked me to come along and do something, so I did stand-up and I was amazed that the audience was very mixed and very varied. I was old enough to be most people's grand-father, like. And I couldn't believe the reaction, I said to myself, 'Jesus, I'm going back to do this again.' I miss the buzz off it now, you see. I just got a little taste of it a few months ago, but it won't be probably until later on in the year or something.

T: So what did you do before d'Unbelievables?

JK: I was arsing around! I wasn't really, I started doing stand-up back in the 80s. I got a mad fit to do stand-up comedy and I remember I was thrown out of places and places were blessed after me leaving, blessed because I was in them!

I used to do this sketch about being born and being in the womb. And it was, like, me just before I was born and I was having a great time inside the womb, and then the experience of being born and the trauma, just what the fuck was going on! You know, no one told me you're going to be conceived, I used to go through all that, the first time I met my father he came into the nursing home he was like me, he couldn't walk, he couldn't talk, we had an awful lot in common – I was just born and he was pissed, basically – so mad stuff.

I did that for a good few years, and I enjoyed it. Like, it was kind of out there, I used to play the guitar and sing. Before that, I started off with a band. We went off to London and we played all the way through the circuit. There wasn't much of a circuit around Ireland, we used to play dancehalls, any place that would have us. And we tried and it didn't work. We got a record deal, we went to London but, you know, we never became famous but sure we had a great experience, seven fellas sleeping in a van. You went on tour with a sleeping bag, if you're lucky enough to have one, and you slept in the van. It was very romantic – you'd be recording in Abbey Road one day, or you'd be in some recording studio with somebody famous, but you hadn't a penny. But it was all great, it was all an experience. But after nine years of that, you suddenly realize that maybe I should try something different, you know.

T: What was the name of the band?

JK: The band was called Gimik. Yeah. The taxi driver who drove me here, he remembered me this evening.

T: He remembered the band?

JK: He did, but he was older than me, like. I think he's retired and he bought a taxi, you know one of these lads? Probably a guard or something!

T: What type of music you'd play?

JK: Ah, we did covers, we did everything, and we were trying to write our own stuff. We didn't know what we were doing. We hadn't a clue, like! Jesus, we hadn't a note. We were talented, but we had no direction because our manager was into greyhounds, you could write a book on it. He was more into greyhounds than he was into music, and sometimes you'd be coming back from a gig and you'd get a phone call, 'Could you collect four greyhounds at Limerick Junction?' We thought we were cool, trendy young fellows, like greyhounds! So it was all a bit crazy.

We got a publishing deal, but it just didn't happen and that's because we didn't have any direction. We know that now. We had no one to crack the whip and say, 'Stop doing that shite and just do this, because you can do this.' So it's important that you have the right kind of coaching or the right mentors when you're doing anything. We'd look back at it now and laugh, because that's all you can do; you can't say, 'Jaysus, I wasted nine years of my life and it never worked out.' We had nine years, it was mad shit, great craic. We travelled, we saw, we gigged, we had fun together, we had a great friendship, we developed a great camaraderie between us, and we're still friends to this day.

T: What are the other lads doing? What's the manager doing?

JK: He passed away actually last year. Believe it or not. But he was still at the greyhounds up to the day he passed away, I think.

T: Do any of your kids want to go into the same business?

JK: Well, we only have two, but Leah, yes, she loves music and performance, all that, that's her thing, so best of luck to her. The world is your oyster – once you have that enthusiasm to do something like that, it's amazing, there's a whole energy within that, and especially I see it within young people today and music and the arts. Hopefully, a little bit more confidence than what we had. Even when I came to RTÉ first I found it totally frightening back in the 80s because it just was too much of an institution for me. Like going back into school, and everyone was so official and it was the national broad-caster. That's all gone now. I mean, our kids, they'd say, 'What's RTÉ?' So the whole narrative has changed, and for the better, I think. It's a great time for them, and there's a huge amount of talent out there and they all support one another. Through the music, through the visual arts, every-thing they're doing, they're all collaborating together.

T: My recollection of your stand-up was that it was 'out there'. It was almost like if you released a pigeon into a room, and just watching it bate around the place. And I get the sense from you that you are kind of one of those people, you're born for a crowd.

JK: Yeah, probably. I never minded it. I fell into it. I never thought I would get into comedy, but when I came to Dublin I was hoping to do a bit of acting after the band. Between the band and the acting and other things, I went away and I joined a dance company for four years. For the craic! Sure I had nothing else to be doing! Better than hanging around with greyhounds! So I did that, and I saw lovely things through that because we went off to Edinburgh and the States and there was a whole new load of influences coming in at me. The punk thing had left an influence on theatre which was young and vibrant.

I love European theatre, I love physical theatre, and I think I brought an awful lot of that definitely, when I was even just playing the guitar with me. You know, I'd just go, 'Let the head off and go wherever it takes you.' And you do it because you're naïve, and that's when I sat back and started to think about it. I remember I came here years ago to RTÉ to record something for some *TV Gaga* programme and they wouldn't show it after I recorded it because they said it was too over the top. And I said, 'I'm only a lad from Limerick.' Like, how could they be over the top, like? But it was savage all right, fairly savage!

T: Could you remember what it was?

JK: It was a doo-wop song based on a fucking car crash . . . great craic, like.

T: Wild.

JK: There was no sense to it – now I know why they were blessing places after me. I had no concept how it might interfere with anyone. I had no barrier, I had no filter, I wasn't editing myself. It was just manic stuff. And I remember one time in New York this guy gave me a review, and he said, 'This guy is like being on speed,' and I suppose I was pretty close to it all right. I've slowed down, but there's still a bit of a kick left in me.

T: There's this great energy in you, and there's still wildness in you.

JK: Jeez, I hope I never lose that. Definitely when the wildness goes you kind of know it's time to hang up the boots. You must always feel as if you never want to lose that kind of madness, like the young giddy heifer on the way to the fair, like, tail cocked in the air . . .

T: . . . and before she knows, she's through the hedge and into another man's land!

JK: That's the one, boy! Well, when you lose that, you're fecked. So it is good to keep that enthusiasm and that energy, and that's all I have anyway, because that kind of covers over for an awful lack of talent.

T: You know, I don't believe that for a moment.

JK: You can get away with murder when you're mad. That's about it, really, because I never got politically involved, although I'm awfully politically aware. I never felt I could ever stand up and say anything that had a political slant to it. It always had to be just about me making a fool of myself or somebody else making a fool of themselves. That madness was probably the backbone of anything I've ever done.

T: From a punter's point of view, though, that's precious. Because there are very few unedited energies out there, so for us to see you like that . . . We put all our madness in a cupboard and we don't look at it, and we need you to express it for us. That's why we love you, Jon, because you're out there and you're fuckin' mad. And I mean that. And what's amazing is to see you now and there's still a sense of that off you.

JK: It is, and it's good for me. I'm very lucky that I have that as a release, that I have some way of leaving off steam out of me or something, otherwise I don't know what I'd do.

T: But it's natural.

JK: Well, I don't know if it is, sometimes you think it's contrived. I would – I think any performer often thinks – like, how much of it is real, where is it coming from? If you overthink it, you wouldn't do it. As I say, I stopped doing it five or six years ago, that sure, maybe I've had enough of this now, and I kind of pulled back from it as well. I didn't want to push myself, I wasn't interested in doing things, whereas now that break has given me a bit more energy. I'm gonna give it another shot, like. I think I'd like to go back out and just throw stuff out to people again and see what happens . . . and hopefully get paid for it.

T: I'm curious about when you got sick. Were you close to the pearly gates and all that? Did you feel that?

JK: Yeah . . . I think you find things. I don't know did I find things or did things find me, but it's amazing. I never talk much about it like that, because there are very personal things and some people probably think that you're mad or well outside of the stage carry-on. I had some tremendous experiences in the sense that I would say that they were actually healing experiences completely. I was very lucky, because I was surrounded with people who did believe in a sort of sense that the healing from other people is really, really strong and good. People call it different things – universal energy, Reiki, mindfulness, whatever you want to call it. It's all about this energy which we have and we give out and other people give out and how we use that.

I remember being in a room one day, and there was four people in the room with me and the whole room just exploded in white light and I just started to cry and stuff started to come out my nose, and I couldn't stop. And they just all went away and they left me alone. One person came back into the room and just said to me, 'I think your healing has started now.' And that was kind of scary, because I didn't know what was happening. You know, when people talk about spiritual experiences, I'm not a church-goer, but I do believe in people, and we all do our best and I believe in good energies. And that happened to me twice, but I've never actually even mentioned this to anyone in a newspaper interview at the time seventeen years ago, because I was afraid to, I didn't have the courage.

Things just happened to me, and I don't know whether I was encouraging them. But I remember one day going to a rugby match in Thomond Park and 'twas that great match where Munster won and O'Gara kicked that point against Gloucester. And I never forget the atmosphere on the ground that day. I said to myself, 'If I could stay here,' and when everyone was gone, I hid and I came back out and I sat in the old stand and I just kept my hands out – it was one of the few times I went to Thomond Park and I wasn't drinking, I'll tell you – and I just sat there for I don't know how long.

And Margie rang me, and she said, 'You probably staying in town tonight?' And I was going through treatment at the time on chemo. And she said, 'I won't see you for two days now.' You know – off out, the lads won, we'd be celebrating. She says, 'Where are you?' I said, 'I'm in Thomond Park.' 'You're still there?' I arrived home at around half ten that night or whatever time it was, and she says, 'You're back?!'

But that's what I was doing, I was just sitting down inside it because the energy from everyone that was there that day was such an occasion and it was such positive energy. I just wanted to sit there and try and get what was left of it into my body. I was holding my hands out – like, if anyone saw me! But this is the first time I have ever spoken about this to anyone, even interviews or anything, even after it, because I suppose I didn't have the confidence and you think, like, this sounds a bit daft or a bit mad, but I do believe it was all part of my living, my healing, my growing.

T: It makes sense.

JK: Well, to me it does, yes, really, it does. It's a necessary thing. There's an awful lot of stuff out there like that. I think that we've really moved too far away from that. I find going to matches, 'tis tribal, 'tis pagan, 'tis spiritual, 'tis close to the stone circle or something. It's something that when everyone goes, 'Yes!' without thinking, just that pure joy when euphoria comes into you and you're not thinking about how you're looking or what you're saying and there's fellows hugging you and you're hugging fellows you would never hug, and it just becomes a release, I suppose. And it's very natural. I think we need more of it.

Kellie Harrington

'There's a lot of people who see boxing as just hitting people in the face, but it's not, it's discipline. It instils discipline in a lot of kids, and adults as well. Without that, God knows where I would be now. I could be in prison or on drugs or anything.'

Tommy: Are you a boxer?

Kellie Harrington: Yes.

T: Can you remind me again of why you were in the news most recently?

KH: The World Championships. I was out in India in November and I became World Champion.

T: I remember watching that, and I can't remember what it was that moved me so much about it. Can you tell us a bit of your back story? I remember when that happened being very taken by you and your story.

KH: I'm twenty-nine now, but I've been boxing since I was roughly fourteen or fifteen, and living in the shadows for many years and not getting the opportunities. I've been training and working at the same time, and eventually got to go for the World Championships in 2016, and I got myself a silver medal then. From there, people started to take me a bit more serious, so I just kept carrying on and getting European medals, and then dropped the weight to sixty kilos, which is an Olympic weight. I got a gold medal in the [2018] World Championships just gone. A massive, massive thing.

The feeling of it is just amazing, for all the work that you put in. You're knocking on the door for years and years, and people doubting you for years, saying, 'She's good, but she's not *that* good like.' Lucky enough that I never listened to any of them. Just kept going, and here I am now.

T: What were you working at while you were training?

KH: Well, I'm still working – in St Vincent's Hospital in Fairview. It's a psychiatric hospital. I'm a household worker so I give out the dinners to the patients, or I could be cleaning. Today, I was in scrubbing toilets this morning. It keeps you grounded, and I love it. I'm on the top bracket of funding now and so I don't actually have to work any more, but it's my escape from boxing. Isn't that great? I can go into a psychiatric hospital and it can take me back to normality!

T: I suppose, in a psychiatric hospital, nobody's pretending to be anything other than what they are.

KH: Exactly. So I fit right in.

T: How did you end up getting a job in a psychiatric hospital?

KH: I just left my CV in . . .

T: Centra or psychiatric hospital . . . !

KH: I got a letter a few weeks later saying I got an interview, so I went up and wham-bam-thank-you-ma'am – ten hours every two weekends! From that, I was then getting called in all the time to cover here and there.

T: What was the work when you got hired?

KH: Cleaning. But now I just give out the dinners. I also do a bit of cleaning, like, if someone phones in sick and I'm not training – I'll go in and put the hours in. It's what I like to do. It just feels like I'm going in to visit people, really. I don't know if much work gets done at all, to be honest with you. I love the patients. There's nine of them in the ward that I'm on. I know them all and they all know me, and we're literally like family.

T: What are they like?

KH: They're very supportive. They'd be always watching me. On my homecoming there when I came back from the World Championships, they were all sitting front row and were straight up to the stage after. And they were all told not to get any ideas in front of the telly or in the paper or anything! Next of all, one of them is up, like, 'GIMME A LOOK AT THAT MEDAL!! GIMME A LOOK!', pulling it from around my neck. Then I'm coming into work a week later and he comes over to me, like, 'Kellie, I got a free coffee last week. Think they noticed me from off the telly!' Yeah, it's great. They're getting something out of my boxing as well. They'll be watching this now and they'll be absolutely buzzing.

T: This show is big in psychiatric hospitals . . . Can you tell me a bit more about the patients and what are they suffering from?

KH: All different kinds of things – schizophrenia, bipolar . . . I wouldn't know what each patient is suffering from, I just know that they're suffering. And out of everyone, they're pretty all right with me because I'm not giving them their medication or taking them for showers or anything like that. I'm coming in and I'm handing them out cigarettes and chocolates and crisps and fizzy drinks. I don't know whether they're glad that I'm a World Champion or just that I'm there giving them treats and what have you.

T: Do some of them think that you might be another patient? 'See your one there, she thinks she's a World Champion . . .'

KH: You know what? They probably do! The craic does be great, though, in there. I don't care what anybody says. Everybody has mental health issues. I have more issues than *Vogue* magazine, for God's sake! So it's pretty sweet going in there. Brings me back down to earth and keeps my feet planted firmly on the ground.

T: When you were growing up, who was the person who directed you most in boxing?

KH: I have three brothers. They would have been sporty. One of my brothers lives in Iceland. He's a soccer coach. I was hanging around with them and getting up to all kinds of mischief. I was the worst possible child you could ever imagine. Drinking, fighting, etcetera. I could always fight and knew I was good at it. But I had to change – I couldn't keep putting me Ma and Da through what I was putting them through, going around looking for me every night. So there were boxing clubs all over the inner city, where I'm from. I got into one of the local boxing clubs and just started training there and kept going. They didn't actually think I was going to stick it out, and to be honest with you, I didn't either. But the discipline from boxing is just amazing. I really looked forward to going.

I had different kinds of friends there with different visions and goals in life. When I first started, it wasn't to become a world champion or an Olympic champion or anything, it was just to do something different. Just a few years at it, the penny finally dropped that I was actually decent, because I never had the confidence in myself. Coaches would be telling me I was good and should fight that person, etcetera, but I was, like, 'No, no, no, they're far too good for me.' But I decided to give it a lash and see how it went. And I am now a changed woman. There's a lot of people who see boxing as just hitting people in the face, but it's not, it's discipline. It instils discipline in a lot of kids, and adults as well. Without that, God knows where I would be now. I could be in prison or on drugs or anything.

T: Are there girls you knew growing up that ended up that way?

KH: Yeah, there would be a few on drugs now. Not many of them – many had kids and moved on. I'm just doing my thing. I don't go out any more, really. I'm not a loner, by any means, but I'm just very driven and I have my sights set on what I want.

T: You don't feel as though you've lost out on anything, like?

KH: No, I don't. And I haven't. There's life after boxing as well. I can catch up on all that kind of craic when I'm finished. But I have something to do. I'm on a mission now.

T: What's that mission?

KH: I want to try and qualify for the Tokyo Olympics. If I qualify for that, I'd probably have a heart attack! But if I qualify, that would be amazing. It'd be great for me, for my family, for my club and for the north-east inner city as well. I'm an ambassador there now for the north-east inner city and that's just absolutely brilliant.

T: What do you have to do in order to qualify?

KH: The World Championships are in Siberia so I have to come in the top four. And because I'm World Champion, I'm the target, I'm the one that people want to beat. People are going to be training to beat me. So it's going to get harder and harder. You have to be 100 per cent mentally prepared. That's one of the biggest aspects of the game – you can be physically fit and everything, but if you're not mentally prepared or if your timing is off and your breathing is gone, the mental side of it is the challenging part.

T: Tell me about that mental preparation?

KH: Really believing in yourself, for one. I have a book, and I write down all my sessions, what I've been doing in my training, who I've been sparring with, how I've been feeling after them. 'Got battered today,' 'Terrible. I need to change this up,' etcetera. Then I look back on that coming up to my competition, when sometimes you'll doubt yourself, thinking you haven't done enough work. If that's written down, then you can look back on it and that's uplifting. Then there's things like, I'm thinking about am I the predator or the prey. This is how we do it with the sports psychologists. It's about acting as well. You have to go in there like, 'I am the champion and I'm going to win this fight.' Even if you don't believe it, you at least have to act it out and go through the motions.

T: Eyeballing your opponent?

KH: Yeah, I don't know . . . they eyeball me back and it doesn't have any effect on me! I was told that I look like Darth Vader when I'm walking into the ring. I was like, 'Thanks very much!' I just switch off, because it's crazy. It's such an adrenaline rush when you walk in, I'd be talking to myself, like, hitting myself. 'Come on, let's go!' The minute you get into that ring you forget about what you have been saying two seconds ago. It's the best feeling ever. Except for when you get hit in the face.

T: I'm very curious about the start of the fight, the first few punches.

KH: Before, we used to do four two-minute rounds. Now we do three threes. People were saying there's a lot more time now for you to settle down and pick your shots. It's still a high pace, but if you make a mistake in the first minute you still have another two minutes to correct that mistake.

T: What would be classified as a mistake?

KH: Getting hit! Say we go out and I throw a jab, like, and they slip and counter with a right hand, I do it again and I get caught again, well, I have to cop on now: 'Don't keep trying that bloody jab because she's slipping and she's catching it every time.' You correct that so you're letting on to throw the jab. She's gonna throw the right hand. You'll move back and catch her again. That kind of stuff.

T: I'm just fascinated because you very rarely get to hear boxers being specific . . . so can you talk me through that thing of what you're throwing when you're throwing it.

KH: Well, they say it's about technique, but they're now sometimes scoring a boxer who's just coming forward and just trying punches. Whether she's landing or not, she's the aggressor. You could be on the back foot and picking her and picking her and picking her, but it might not be what the judges want to see any more. Technically, you have to be nice and relaxed and picking your shots. It's like a game of chess. I'm just used to seeing things before they come, just reading someone's body if they throw something, to just step back and miss the punch. The technical side of it is brilliant.

T: Who out there is good now in your weight division?

KH: The Russian – couldn't tell you her name! The Finnish girl, Mira Potkonen. I know her because she's beaten me twice, but it's getting closer each time. And then the girl from Thailand [Sudaporn Seesondee]. I met her in the final of the 2018 World Championships. She's good. Hits like a horse. She looks like one as well! Ah no, she's good. They're all good. Everyone is a threat, really. It's all 'on the day', as well.

Mentally, you have to be prepared and ready to go to war but change it up if you need to. In the final of the World Championships, I lost the first round. It's hard to come back after losing your first round. But I got to the final in 2016 and I had settled – not, like, I had *settled*, but I didn't go in thinking like, I'm going to lose this, like – but I didn't do what I could have done. I had so much more left in the tank to perform and I didn't do it and I got out of the ring and I was like, 'Why didn't I?' This time, after the first round, I came back to the corner. The coach – I knew by his face.

I says, 'What's the story?'

He says, 'Very, very close.'

But very, very close doesn't mean it's a split decision in the first round. It's mad, the way you think, because you get a one-minute break in between the rounds and it's crazy what you can think in that minute, really quickly. I was thinking, I'm not settling for this, this is not what I came out here for. If I lose, I want to at least be able to say I gave it everything. So I just went out and started to use the jab a lot more, and began landing them and getting lighter on my feet. She was getting really frustrated, and the more frustrated she got, I was getting more cocky, moving more and countering her every time she was coming. I won the next two rounds.

T: How much does that take out of you? Like, what kind of reserves are you drawing on in order to lift your game? How much heart? You're in the first round, it hasn't gone well, but you've obviously still been trying. How much more did you have to try to win rounds two and three?

KH: I just have to come alive. Start throwing more punches and stop being as cautious. And start letting my hands go, really. You have to work, like. Like, you're going into the last round and you know, I've been here, I've had these spars [in training]. I've done the work. I can definitely do this. There's only two rounds left like two rounds you could be world champion. So I went out and I kinda just picked it up, and I knew I had it in me. I had so much more left in the tank. Now, come the end of the round, the end of the fight, I was absolutely on my feet, and it was a split decision, three–two – three judges gave it to me and two gave it to her. I just couldn't believe it then. I couldn't believe it – like, mentally, I was actually able to change after the first round.

T: You're obviously someone who is capable of change, in mid-fight and mid-life as well.

KH: Change is good, but everything is good for me now. I'm not looking for any more change, except for possibly an Olympic medal. That might be nice to add to my collection.

T: All this hard training, all this hard fighting, and yet you're still going into the psychiatric hospital to clean up and to talk to people and to befriend outsiders, and like you said earlier, you don't know what they're suffering from but you know they're suffering.

KH: But everybody's suffering, aren't they? In some way, shape or form, everybody is suffering. But it's about how you manage it. For me, boxing and the exercise is great for mental health. If I didn't have it, I don't know what I'd do. Boxing is my medication.

Lynn Ruane

'It's not about giving [children] hope, because
you can have hope for the rest of your life
and still have nothing.'

Tommy: So, Lynn, would you tell me who you are?

Lynn Ruane: Ah, the ego's going to take a bruising, is it? You don't know who I am!

T: No, I'm sorry.

LR: OK, my name is Lynn Ruane, I'm from Tallaght, I'm a senator, I'm on the Trinity panel – I was voted in by Trinity graduates. We've something in common – my name is Ruane which is Mayo.

T: Like the Tiernans, yeah.

LR: And my only Tommy Tiernan story is, and you can correct me if I'm wrong, but I think you had a relation in the same ward as my dad was many years ago.

T: In the psychiatric?!

LR: Basically! No, I don't know whether it was an uncle or a father-in-law or something, but you used to come into the ward to visit somebody, and my dad had dementia and I remember saying, 'There's Tommy Tiernan,' and my dad used to say, 'I have dementia, but I'm not stupid. That is not Tommy Tiernan!'

T: My father-in-law had a stroke and was in Tallaght hospital for a while.

LR: There ya go.

T: How did you end up being a senator?

LR: Well, I worked in the community sector for a long time in addiction. I developed addiction programmes since I was about seventeen. I left school fairly young and I started . . .

T: Sorry, hold on a second – you started developing addiction programmes when you were seventeen?

LR: Yes.

T: How does that happen?

LR: I left school at fifteen and I done a two-year course in An Cosán. I became a mother at fifteen, and me and my daughter attended there. It was developed by Katherine Zappone and Ann-Louise Gilligan. It's like a community education project in Tallaght, which is still going strong. They had childcare so I was able to go and re-enter education as a young mother and have my daughter with me. So from there, I went and I done a . . .

T: Fifteen, like.

LR: Yeah, fifteen.

T: I was twenty-four when I had my first child and I feel as if . . . not that we grew up together, but that I matured so much having him.

LR: Well, me and Jordanne definitely grew up together!

T: Hang on – did you tell your parents that you were pregnant?

LR: Straight away. I'm not good with secrets, I'm not good with lying. When something's up against me, I kind of don't dodge it, I just go full force at it . . .

T: That's how you [got pregnant] . . .

LR: I won't disagree!

T: I didn't say it, though, did I?

LR: You didn't have to! Ma, don't mind him!

T: I'm stunned by that. Was there ever a thought of not bringing up the baby yourself or anything like that?

LR: No, there wasn't. I had two very supportive parents and, obviously, it wasn't ideal for them at the time, but like they did with every stage of my life, they wrapped their support around me and made it much easier. And I had a wide circle of friends and lots of family on the father's side as well, who all helped, so I wasn't alone. Obviously, there are lots of young mothers who wouldn't have been in that same situation and I'm always very conscious of them, but I was lucky.

T: And then you're back in the education system.

LR: I was in An Cosán for two years and then I did an addiction studies programme in IT Tallaght. It was one evening a week.

T: Why did you choose addiction studies?

LR: Because it would have been very hit and miss whether I would have ended up in addiction myself. I would have been recreationally using drugs since a very young age. My friends had all begun heroin just as I became pregnant, so it could have gone either way for me. I wanted to find a way that I could support and help and empower people within my own community to look at addiction and heroin use and how we can challenge that.

T: Even though you're only a child yourself and you have a two-year-old baby, you're inspired to do that?

LR: I was inspired to do it, and it wasn't easy because there was probably that part of me that wanted to still go and use drugs and party and go out! So I was trying to balance letting go of my childhood and my friends, in a sense, in what direction that they were taking, and maybe I felt that the only way I could stay close to them was to be involved with drugs in another sense. I spent a lot of time trying to understand why communities like mine had so much addiction in them.

T: And why do they?

LR: Inequality. People will say addiction doesn't know any postcodes, but chaotic, problematic drug use does. Addiction looks very different in working-class communities than it does in more affluent communities, and our response to it in working-class areas, where we don't have the support or the safety nets, looks very different too. Now I wouldn't have had an understanding beyond Tallaght at the time, but the more I pursued my education and worked in Trinity, I really began to understand the idea of class and the impact that social class can have.

T: What happened after your studies?

LR: Well, entering the addiction studies course was actually quite difficult because I was so young. At the time, a local community woman that ran the course kind of forced the hand of the course coordinator to let me in. The other coordinator, Father Liam O'Brien, who developed drugs courses in Killinarden, came to me at the end of the course and apologized for not thinking that I would be able for it and offered me a job to develop a programme for young heroin users in my own community. I wouldn't have been too far ahead of them, to be honest – they would have been thirteen, fourteen, fifteen, and I was only a couple of years older. From there, he offered me a second job to be the outreach worker for the cocaine project. That would have been the first cocaine initiative in the country and a very different style of work to what I'd been doing around heroin users and methadone, because it was a recreational drug. People didn't really want to associate with methadone clinics.

T: I imagine you've seen a lot of lives destroyed?

LR: A lot of lives destroyed. Even in my own life. Even though now I'm in the Seanad, I'm still very much integrated in my own community and still have the friends that I went to school with. You get halfway through the year and you're going, 'Has no one died yet?' I really believe that our social classes are killing us, whether it be through addiction, mental health, suicide or even risk-taking, just having so little value on your life or aspirations or thinking that you're not going to live very long anyway. So you're much more risky in your behaviour, which sometimes can cost you your life. Both in my work and in my personal life, death would be quite a permanent feature.

T: And does it break your heart to see that stuff?

LR: It does break my heart, but it drives me. Every time I stand in the Seanad, I talk about things in abstract. A lot of my stuff is about gender, around addiction and around homelessness. I worked in the homeless sector as well for a long time. I try to package it and articulate it in a way that those in politics will understand. So when I stand in the chamber I try and not let it break my heart any more, because I'd be just crying all the time. Over the past few years I became a story – the girl from a working-class community in Killinarden who became President of Trinity College Student's Union and got a Seanad seat – and I suppose change will only ever be evident if people don't see me as a story any more and it becomes pretty normal for people like me to be in the positions that I'm in. I can only try in my little part to make some of that change, but I definitely can't completely overhaul the system to be any different.

T: Is there savage inequality in Ireland?

LR: Massive. And my fear is that not everybody under-stands it completely. Some people ridicule and personalize attacks on politicians when they don't understand inequality, but for me, I believe if we've all been reared and are in differ-ent situations of our lives, we're all looking at the same thing from a different view and we need to be able to talk to each other. Some people understand privilege and how it has given them an advantage. But then there's other people that have privilege and they don't understand it, in the exact same way that we have oppression and inequality by moral luck – where you're born, your postcode. That's complete luck.

T: Talk me through it. Give me an example of a family in an underprivileged situation and tell me what those people go through and what they have to deal with.

LR: OK, so you could take a young child going to school in Tallaght. Maybe they come from a one-parent household, maybe there's six or seven children in that household or maybe there's only one. Maybe there's addiction in the household, domestic violence. The parent probably only has second-level education, they really want their child to survive . . .

T: Can I interrupt you there? See, when you phrase it like that, the language is almost too factual. What I'm trying to hear is: a child wakes up in the morning, the mother's first urgency is to score some heroin, the father beats the mother, the child is there, is there enough food . . . To break it down into human language that I can understand. You're not talk-ing to a journalist or a politician here, so give me some examples.

LR: I suppose why I have learnt to put it in those terms is because when I talk about families, I'm probably drawing on my experience with a particular family and I never, obviously, want to highlight that. You're talking about kids that watch their parents score drugs, who have had to witness their father batter their mother to a pulp first thing in the morning and then go to school and be expected to sit in a classroom and give a shit about maths and Irish when they've just come with a schoolbag full of trauma into that classroom.

I could give a million examples, but I'm hesitant to and afraid to because I don't want to hit on anyone's real story and for them to be thinking, is she talking about me here?

Working-class families are often seen as, 'they don't care about the child's education,' but if you're a working-class mother, your sole thing is that your child doesn't end up in criminality, addiction, leaving school at twelve and going off and robbing cars and shops. How can you care about the Leaving Cert or third-level education when you're just trying to get your child past certain milestones that means they'll stay alive?

People don't understand that we care about education and we care about our kids succeeding but we're firefighting really hard situations every day. They talk about that there's no starvation any more because of the welfare system, but if you went into some of the homes in some of the poorest areas in this country, there's absolutely nothing.

To give an example, I done a piece of research a few years back with middle-ranking drug-dealers. One young man in that research who entered drug-dealing said that there was ten of them in the family and they had no cutlery. There were so many of them he used to have to eat his cornflakes out of the sink. He used to put the stopper in the sink and put the milk and the cornflakes in the sink and eat his corn-flakes from there before he went to school. And the very first reason he sold drugs as a kid, maybe hash or something, was because he didn't want to wear any more hand-me-downs from his brothers – he was the youngest. When you're growing up in a situation like that, your choices can become what the rest of society wants to look down on but don't really understand where them choices are coming from, when you have a kid who says, 'I don't want to wear my brothers' hand-me-downs any more, I want my own tracksuit.'

T: Do you feel that power in Ireland is able to change that, that there are people that can change that?

LR: I do. I think we all can change it. When we look at every society, there's always going to be the haves and the have-nots. But that's just the default position because they actually don't want to do anything about it. Education was my biggest liberator, and if we found ways to make education much more holistic in working-class areas, there could be greater access for kids to enter university. Small things like changing the curriculum, looking at continuous assessment for Leaving Cert, looking at their skill sets, looking at the teachers. If teachers in working-class communities did their work experience in the local youth club or addiction centre or traveller centre, rather than doing them in Deis schools, they might have a bit more understanding of the kids that they're working with.

T: Is it hope, Lynn? Is it about giving children hope?

LR: It's not about giving them hope, because you can have hope for the rest of your life and still have nothing. It's about levelling out the playing field and not making university and certain types of employment too far out of reach for kids from areas like mine. When I was younger, I told my mam that I wanted to be a vet, and my mam said, 'Oh, yeah I think I know someone that might have been a vet before,' and was wracking her brain wanting to tell me what I needed to do.

That's how little information we have. But if you're in a more affluent area, it's not only about finance or income, it's about your social and cultural-capital connections. So if I'm in a more affluent area and I go, 'Mam, I'd love to be a vet,' she'd say, 'Oh, hang on, and I'll ring so-and-so's daughter, she's a vet. Maybe she'd give you your work experience.' It's not always about finance, it's about connections as well. We all could make an effort to integrate ourselves into working-class areas and look at kids who are doing their work experience in the local shop when they'd much prefer to do it with an engineer and not batter the aspirations out of them.

T: Do you come into contact with the people who actively ruin communities?

LR: Yeah. Do I believe that they wake up in the morning and go out to actively ruin communities? No, I don't. I remember the late Ann Louise Gilligan saying that everything is an educational process. I just wish that the people that are in power would allow us to bring them on that educational process so they can have real understanding. There's some people in power that think they could have been born in Jobstown and still be running the country. If I was to have my way, I'd probably bring in class quotas and make sure that there was a seat for someone from the migrant community, the travelling community, etcetera, and really diversify politics so that it's much more representative. The moment it becomes more representative, you will see policies shift. In working-class communities, we need to make more of an effort to vote – if we do, politics and policies will have to be dragged in the other direction because all of a sudden we're worth something. But if we don't vote, then they can ignore us all they want because they're not threatened by us, and I think we need to be threatening them.

T: It's such an awful sadness to see young people in situations where their options seem to be limited and the odds are against them from a very young age.

LR: Extremely sad. People talk about choice like, 'Well, you chose to take drugs,' or 'You chose to go down that road.' But if you're a ten-year-old child and you're looking around you, you don't know any pilots or dentists or doctors or engineers, none of your neighbours are any of those things. Is that really a choice? Your choice is diluted by what you're looking around at. We don't really have free will, often, in working-class areas. Sometimes I'm used, like, 'If she made it, so can you.' But I had many interventions along the way – An Cosán, a supportive family, a mother who read to me since the moment I was born, you know? If I was to look at privilege and oppression in a working-class area, I was probably fairly privileged because I did have a safety net and support all around me. There was no addiction in the family, no violence. My choices cannot be used as some sort of example.

Michael D. Higgins

*'The fact of the matter is: as long as you're
drawing breath, stay curious and keep going.
That's what you do.'*

Michael D. Higgins: Well, there we are.

Tommy: One of my best friends.

MDH: Thank you. It's shared.

T: Where have you been recently?

MDH: Well, I was at Auschwitz at a memorial service for those who were murdered in those atrocious conditions. Probably that's the last trip abroad that I was on. Most of the next few weeks and months are incoming trips and so on. I went to the ceremonies and then the following day I visited the Jewish district in Krakow and also visited some of the new initiatives that they have where Jewish people and non-Jewish people are coming together to, if you like, re-create an atmosphere in Krakow that is welcoming to all groups.

T: So what's in the Jewish district now?

MDH: Well, the tragedy of the whole thing is that it was of course a heavily populated Jewish centre in the city of Krakow, and they were brought to the different concentration camps and eliminated. And then what you have now is, if you like, a building-back of a community and also something else as well that was very important – people recalling and remembering and researching their Jewish identity in

quite a modern way. And I visited one of the oldest synagogues that had been there since the sixteenth century. There
were altogether about six synagogues in a small space. The
narrative of what happened is striking.

T: There seems to be a lot of talk nowadays about the rise
of anti-Semitism again. It's not something that I'm familiar
with, and I'm astounded by it, but the voices are fervent that
it's happening again. Do you have a sense of it arising again?

MDH: I do, and I think, unfortunately, part of it is just
simply a hatred and suspicion of minorities, and that is something that we have to really address. What do I mean by that?
I think that it's very, very important to realize that all these
camps and Auschwitz and others didn't fall from the skies.
Maybe what struck me in my memory as I was listening to
the presentations was that in 1938 at the Évian Conference,
not a single country would take any [Jewish refugees]. It is
important to realize that the nations of the world, including
some of the richest – and this goes for the ship that sailed to
the United States that wasn't allowed to land – there is a con-
sciousness of nations having closed their doors. As one of
the speakers put it at the Auschwitz ceremony, the only country that said they would accept anybody was the Dominican
Republic, and there's that.

But then, more importantly, what I think about it as well
is it's very important to realize the sources of the anti-
Semitism, which go way back. In fact, it's one of the most
interesting things in relation to those of us interested in literature and philosophy. Both the Jews and Islamic scholars
who translated Aristotle were in their day expelled from
Spain by Isabella, which was, quite frankly, on the grounds
of pursuing the true faith to share bigotry and exclusion. So
it is ancient, and within what's happening it is very important

to realize how it was built up. For example, it began with differences in the parks, with park benches where Jewish people weren't allowed to sit, where you began making separations in the community and in the society. And I think all of this is important, Tommy, because as you know, for the last couple of years, I've been working very much on speeches about memory and speeches about how to handle the past and how do you do it in a way that doesn't make you impotent in the present or lose opportunities in the future. But I was very moved by that visit I went on. That's a long answer to your question.

T: What's the connection between having a view on Israel and Palestine while at the same time checking yourself for prejudice?

MDH: I think that point is very important. Many of us, for example, would from time to time have condemned breaches of international law. The settlements in the West Bank are illegal. In my previous life, when I went very often to Palestine Gaza, I felt it was tragic how little progress was being made towards establishing some kind of model in which people could live together. What I think was very much striking was the effects on women and children in that part of the world, but also other parts of the world. I looked at a psychological study of the impact on children of seeing their parents humiliated, and the thing about it is that humiliation had a deeper traumatic effect on the majority of the children that had lost either parent. Without justice, if you like, anti-Semitism, along with other forms of exclusion and hatred, come quickly and without hesitation.

But it is equally important in relation to trying to see a peaceful resolution in the area that is Palestine, Israel and the whole region, that you must remain free to make your criticisms on the basis of what is proper. Some months ago, when I was in the Lebanon and visited four huge camps there, the Palestinian people there were effectively locked away, stateless people. So it is one of the great failures of diplomacy, and I think one of the reasons it has failed is because people haven't stayed with it with sufficient mechanisms for making proposals. Obviously, I have to be careful what I say now so I don't interfere with government business. I know that some people have worked very hard on it, but usually what happens is that you have an initiative, it perishes, and then you're starting all over again. I don't see it as hopeless at all. I think there are initiatives that can be taken.

T: In terms of Ireland, in terms of Europe, what scandalizes you at the moment?

MDH: Well, I don't use words like 'scandalize' at the moment. Maybe I've gone through it. But you must let me add to what I've been saying, to finish from the previous part we've been discussing now. The important thing is we must never be indifferent. The rise of racism, the rise of anti-Semitism, the suffering of people in these humiliations – the moral absolute is how did it happen, for example, in relation to the Second World War, that you could have had these conferences years in advance, that you could see all of this coming? And the answer was that people were indifferent. We can't be indifferent again.

But when you come to where we are now, I think that in Ireland, and in many places, what has happened is that there's a kind of a 'catastrophe of feeling', as one writer I know puts it. It is that people feel distant from the institutions that are taking decisions about them. It's the distinction between two different campaigns about democracy. One is a kind of a liberal democracy, where everyone is free to pursue their own interest, and the idea is that you do so and you'll resolve conflicts. The other is a kind of a republican view of democracy where you assume that there is a common good that affects us all, and therefore the way you proceed is through other people.

If you take the second path, you'll put a lot of value on the public world, on public spaces, on the things that are shared in common. What has happened in many cases is that the very basics by which people need to be connected to the society, all the literature screams out at you that the earlier you make interventions in relation to equality for children, the better. The same is true in relation to education. I remember a time when in fact you didn't have free secondary education where I was reared in County Clare. Obviously, the one that is also being debated, and correctly so, is housing.

A Professor Rosa in Germany has written a book called *Resonance* about how do you resonate with the world, how are you taken into the world and how do you take the world into you. And that's where you see all the inequalities showing. It is very possible to address these issues, but what happens in many cases is people are not resonating with the world. You have people who don't, for example, understand what it is that their company makes any more – the older versions of these companies in the history of Europe and elsewhere, back then, you knew you were making something. For example, I remember Tom Murphy the playwright and Mick Brennan talking about which of their mothers made the most kinds of bread, you know? There was something there, you were involved in a real world. But what has happened today is that in many, many ways people are living in a virtual world.

Even, for example, in relation to communications. I was writing about it recently, about all those Saturdays I was protesting for acceptable justice most of my life, you'd know that there would be people of all ages there and they'd be talking to each other as they were going along, and then you had all these banners, and then you had the speech, and then you were talking on the way home again. Now, you can organize an event simply electronically. So suddenly you're living now in a kind of a virtual atmosphere.

Then you get to a point as well where people, for example, would say the markets are good today or the indicators are solid. I'm sure these metrics are very useful, but they're used in a very narrow frame. I know what they mean, but really, what are they saying about the people who are involved? Because you could, for example, as I believe happened in the response after the crash of 2008, have a pursuit of fiscal objectives at the cost of the public, and then what happened?

People really need to know the choices that are open to them, and irrespective of which choice it is, you need to be participating in it. And how can you participate if these matters are too complex for ordinary people to understand? People are alienated, people are disenchanted, and they're wide open to being exploited by people who say, 'Well, it's all the fault of the migrants or that group.'

We're now in a position where we need a kind of economic literacy – and it's not about Ireland or Europe, it's global – so that people are able to participate in decisions that are affecting them in relation to the big issues. And the hopeful side of it, Tommy, is that after all the divisions and failures, there is a great opportunity to bring into existence a project that would be able to unite people who had divided on the basis of belief systems or faiths or nations, in, for example, saving the planet, in relation to responding to climate change, in relation to sustainability.

But you have to stay at it because it requires, in the same way as in physics or anything, a paradigm shift. And what disappoints me very often is that what I describe now is not necessarily being shared in all sections of the academic world. Therefore, how do you prepare for a world in which people will, for example, connect the economy to a responsible relationship to nature, to ecology, to global poverty? How do you bring these three together? That's what I do. But it's a kind of an interesting peasant thing from the time I was in County Clare as a child. I loved books and words when I had the opportunity to be given them, and you know yourself, when something strikes you and you're mad to tell someone about it . . .

T: Are you walking around the Áras now, waking Sabina up?!

MDH: Boring other people! But it's like a new dance, or any of these intellectual ideas, in many cases, there isn't much point in just locking yourself in a cloister. That's why I got involved in all these debates and rows and everything like that. If you'll go to the trouble of acquiring the knowledge, don't you want to share it?

T: It's a compulsion.

MDH: It is.

T: Even if nobody understands you!

MDH: Well, you'd be surprised, actually. I pretend sometimes I don't, because I don't want to hear it, probably! But it's a matter of developing the capacity to listen, and the listening is important. Are you open to alternative ideas in language? And then the biggest one of all is are you open to transforming your own thinking in any way? All of this is very, very important, for example, in relation to what we went through in Northern Ireland, global issues and the

United Nations. You have to take risks. You're taking them very successfully now here. Fair play to you, I must say.

T: In terms of who's coming to the country, who's on their way?

MDH: The President of Portugal is coming in May, so is the President of Germany. And then there may be some of the neighbours . . .

T: Where are *they* now?

MDH: They're still talking to us. Even if they have in fact discovered greatness again . . .

T: When you have these people coming over, do you have notions what you might do with them?

MDH: Well, I'm only a minor part of it. I feed them, for which they pay the price of listening to one of my speeches, and then they propose a toast to my health and happiness and the people of Ireland and their prosperity. Then the Department of Foreign Affairs and Department of the Taoiseach take over. It usually lasts about three days. But, in fairness, the President of Portugal, President de Sousa, is a fine man. He goes swimming every day, you know – fit, that kind of thing. You probably are a daily swimmer yourself?

T: I'm not. No, I tried.

MDH: You stopped, did you?

T: I did it for a week, and for that week I couldn't stop telling everybody I was a daily swimmer. So you don't get to say, 'Oh, I'd love to take the President of Germany to Navan or Tayto Park,' or something?

MDH: Nor Kilbeggan either – there are lots of places. But that's a great idea, that . . . but there would be a security problem!

T: How's your body?

MDH: I'm supposed to say, 'Grand, thank you, and your-self?' I'm fine. I have all these parts that are moving a different way than before, but there's nothing much you can do. These people during the last election tried to tell me I could do something about the ageing process – well, I was very sorry, I couldn't exactly invent a machine to fire myself backwards. No, but thank you, my health is, thankfully, good. Yes.

T: I know from talking to you that you've sometimes found the Áras a lonely place to be at times.

MDH: Yeah. Well, I think if I wasn't a person that read so much it would be hard enough, because very often in the even-ings there's just Sabina and myself and two wonderful dogs, and there is the aide-de-camp, and there's two security always there. But, no, I have to say that the time flew and everyone has been very good to me. I suppose I have missed very, very much the old circles that I moved in before. Maybe it's just as well that some of them I'm not moving in any more!

I'm going to too many funerals of good friends of mine. That's sad. For example, Tom Murphy was a dear friend of mine. Tom and I go way back. Something that's important I think for us all to realize – I think it was Nietzsche that said it – a man wasn't born to be happy; only the English thought that. The fact of the matter is everyone has in their whole cycle of their life different challenges. It's about the sense of empathy. There's nothing more important than that. It is about judging, accepting and welcoming a person for what they are in the fullness of their person as a fellow human being.

T: That sounds more complicated than just saying 'em-pathy', doesn't it?

MDH: It does. Empathy is a fine thing, and you can brand it as empathy if you like, but it is important. Saying not to treat other people in a way that you wouldn't like to be treated your-self, that's a bit limited. I was mentioning Professor Rosa earlier. He makes the case that there is such a thing as the common good. You may differ about the way you're going to achieve it, but the common good should be something that shouldn't be taken for granted if you have option A, option B and options C and D. What gives legitimacy to them as options at all is the notion of the common good, and that is contra-dicted by extreme individualism. That is why it is a nonsense to say, for example, that the populations of the world should submit themselves to the vagaries of the marketplace to solve practically every aspect of human need. That's a nightmare, and it's a nightmare through which we are living now.

T: But who defines 'the common good'? Historically, per-haps, did we have the Church to define what it was?

MDH: Well, there was a time when we knew, and that raises the question, from where do you take authority? There's no doubt whatsoever when you look at all the different peoples of the world in different periods, they've attempted forms of transcendence. Something beyond the self, people who ascribed divinity to trees and Mother Nature and offered the different belief systems. The difficulty is when you get abso-lute claims, when you get a kind of a war between certainties. Why, how and from where are you going to discover 'the inner Republic'? Authority should come from the people, and there shouldn't be a single voice. I have been describing the situation where people feel disconnected from institutions, disconnected from space, where they're living disconnected from different things. The next thing then is for the authori-tarian voice to emerge from the shadows and say, 'I'm going to be your voice.' This is very much what has happened in the United States.

T: And going back to the conversation at the start with Germany in the 1930s.

MDH: Yes. The first thing that happens is you allow people to be rendered mute or to feel in fact that they themselves don't understand what's happening, and then you offer to explain it for them and then what you need is 'the strong man'. That's how it happens . . . So I didn't come on a show to just depress everybody. You should help me along by saying things like, 'That's more like it,' or 'Enough of that now!'

T: Enough of that now!! . . . Now – did you meet Trump?

MDH: No, I haven't had the pleasure yet. I don't play golf.

T: No, you're the wrong shape for golf!

MDH: I beg your pardon! Well, there you are now. I've seen people in worse condition than me going out with clubs!

T: Do you ever go back to Clare and the home house?

MDH: Well, the home house is demolished now, but there's a house in its place that my nephew has built. I do go down. I went down not so long ago to visit my sister. She lives in Shannon. But that house in Ballycar, I went there at the age of five and my brother was four, and I was reared by my aunt and uncle. My poem in one of the collections, 'Katie's Song', is about that wonderful woman. There was one room slated and there was two rooms thatched, and everything was fine, really, while my uncle was able to farm. And then my aunt died, and the thatched roof deteriorated badly, and things went downhill from there. And then my brother and my mother lived in one of those railway cottages just at the gates at Ballycar. People sometimes say to me as if it was some kind of great impoverishment or something, but no, there were many, many wonderful positive things about it – to be reared on a farm for example, and to know about cows and calves, and there was compulsory tillage so there was a lot of ploughing and harvesting going on. But it was by accident that I came through education. When I did the Leaving in 1960 . . .

T: Were you repeating?

MDH: A *fantastic* Leaving, Tommy – Greek and Latin and everything. But I didn't go into the Church. No, at that time you got this thing that the *Irish Independent* had which advertised all of the jobs. I was working in a factory in Shannon and I applied for the ESB. I'm a grade-eight clerk retired. The ESB was my first trade union, but I think it is just as well for the sake of the energy production of the country that I left.

T: I'd hate to see you stuck up a pole in a gale!

MDH: There you are. Actually, I was there during the last phase of rural electrification and we would go out to the country and we'd have a switch-on hooley – the parish priest would lift a sheet from a bulb! After that, I got a loan and then I got scholarships and I'd go to England every summer, which really advanced my 'life skills', if you get me. I was living in a hotel, and so forth. As someone said to me about it all, 'You wouldn't die wondering.' And then I went to the United States and to Manchester, and then I came back and began teaching. And I loved the teaching because it was always the case, as I was saying, that if you had something new, then you want to communicate it. And that's where I am today. For goodness' sake. Miracle, isn't it?!

T: Do you remember that line of Beckett's – 'Perhaps my best years are gone, but I wouldn't want them back. Not with the fire that's in me now.' Do you have that sense of being energized?

MDH: Well, I'm doing good work now. I wish I'd had all of that information earlier on. That's all. But the other side of it, I don't waste my time on. The fact of the matter is: as long as you're drawing breath, stay curious and keep going. That's what you do.

T: You have a remarkable mind. Like, I am amazed at your ability, almost irrespective of the subject I might bring up when we meet personally, to have thirty-three theories about it. You just have a phenomenal, phenomenal intellect. You're shockingly well informed.

MDH: Well, it was one of the things about words and books. When my mother had lost, really, everything in Limerick and we were moving, she'd still go to O'Mahony's bookshop and she'd buy books even in the difficult times, and my uncle and aunt bought the paper and so on. And I didn't go to primary school until I was seven, but I was used as a kind of a 'demonstration' of that whole home education. I learned from the newspaper headlines how to read.

I say all of this only to encourage anyone in the Republic – any child, boy or girl, what I say to them is that where I am now would have seemed impossible at several stages of my life for different reasons, and these things should hopefully inspire. That's what's important, for people to come through these things.

I noticed as well, it's very important to touch people. I was reared separate from my two sisters, wonderful women. They emigrated to England at twenty but my sister now is eighty down in Shannon, Kathleen, with whom I have a very warm relationship still. But I remember when she visited us out in the country and she held my hand going down the road towards Newmarket-on-Fergus, and that was in a time in Ireland in the 1950s when people didn't touch each other.

And that was a great pity, because if there is a history of thought, a history of philosophy, in many cases you look at the great paintings, it's people reaching out to touch each other. Now, of course you do that with tact and with respect, but it's important even you say about the intellectual side of it: 'I was touched by what you said.' Aristotle regarded touch as the most important of the senses. Plato thought that the visual was the most important of the senses and Plato led us all wrong. That was our mistake. We're much better off when we are able, in fact, to engage, with sensibility, with all of the phenomena of the world, dogs and horses and people and everything.

T: Are you touched enough?

MDH: Yeah, I work at it. When I was living in the United States back as a student, when the breaks came and all the students went down to Florida, I was sharing an accommodation with two great Mexican friends. I travelled with them down to Mexico, and I remember when I went over the border into Mexico, the way in which people gave each other *un abrazo* [embrace]. And they did it sort of as part of the culture. It is one of the reasons why, in fact, the world of Latin American people has always been close to my heart. They're just people who concentrate on the very good, the best. They are some of the best dancers in the world and they express their feelings well.

Particularly we owe it to the feminist tradition and the feminist movement in Ireland that had broken down all of that coldness and so forth. Wasn't it a terrible thing to be saying to people that the body is inherently sinful and you should cover yourself up? In Salthill, when I came to Galway first, there was a priest who wouldn't serve Communion to women with sleeveless blouses. We can't have people at that – people putting on cardigans to receive Communion. I mean, what a distortion really of the whole sacrament that Communion is.

T: God became flesh because he loved it.

MDH: Well, he did. Oh, I could rely on you for the theology always. There we are now. Did anything else strike you? Will we get contemplative?

T: When will I see you again?

MDH: Well, you know where I am. They'll never stop you at the gate, Tommy.

Michael Harding

*'I don't feel I'm a wise person that became religious.
I find it like a weakness in me. I look at other
people who are not religious and I admire them,
if not envy them.'*

Michael Harding: How are ya?

Tommy: I'm mighty now. All the better for seeing you. What are you at? Are you going around the place at the minute with a book?

MH: Aye. It's a book called *On Tuesdays I'm a Buddhist*. I don't say what I'm doing Wednesday or Fridays.

T: Will you remind me of the gist of it?

MH: My wife brought me back an icon from Poland. She's not Polish, but she brought back an icon because she was working on icons in the museum. I had given up, really, on the Christian practice a good few years ago. Thirty years ago . . .

T: But you hung on to the clothes, though?

MH: I'm from Cavan . . . I left the priesthood and I left all the Christian thing behind me and I really couldn't live without some experience of faith. And I was coming up to forty and felt I needed psychotherapy. I needed someone to talk to me or listen to me. I didn't have sixty euros to spend on an hour's therapy. There was a Buddhist, a Tibetan Lama living about twenty mile away. I knew that Buddhism wasn't a revealed religion in the same way as Christianity or Islam or Judaism. I knew that Buddhism is a kind of psychotherapy in itself. So I thought, OK, I'll go over to this fella and I'll get into it.

T: It's one of those things where you can participate without having to believe in anything.

MH: Yes. The principles of Buddhism are slightly different, in the sense that there's nothing revealed except that you're offered propositions on various ideas about how the mind works and you're asked to practise them and see if they work for you. And if they don't work for you, then don't worry about them. I needed something, and I found it, a kind of a refuge. So if I wanted to devote myself to lighting candles and looking at holy pictures, I now did it in a kind of Buddhist way. At the start, I didn't really know how to meditate. I used to go over to them and there was a Buddhist nun teaching everybody how to meditate. We'd all be sitting around on a Thursday evening, and she'd say, 'Just breathe in and out,' and 'Just focus, keep the back straight and pick a point at the end of your nose.' But I thought she meant *at* the end of my nose, so I went home and I was practising and I was going cross-eyed!

T: I wonder are we at different stages in our . . .

MH: . . . Development, Tommy.

T: Well, that's an awful term to use. I wonder are we similar? I would look up to you an awful lot, Michael, and I've said this to you before. Often after talking to you onstage, I'd find myself impersonating you. But I wonder are we at different stages of our journey? If the journey is towards anywhere, I don't know. I have found myself recently being very drawn to Catholicism and very drawn to Jesus and God, the Bible, Gospels, and even though I know in some way I'm pretending, I find that in my heart it does make sense. So when your wife came back with the icon, did it reawaken old desires or something?

MH: What happened when I got the icon is I started spending a long time looking at it and then I thought that maybe I should really get rid of all of this religiosity. I feel it was a mistake, I don't feel it as a wisdom, I don't feel I'm a wise person that became religious. I find it like a weakness in me. I look at other people who are not religious and I admire them, if not envy them. But I love the smell of incense and candles, I just like it. So I thought in the book I'd say, 'Well, I need to cleanse myself of all of this.' I went down to Cill Rialaig [Arts Centre] in Kerry and went out to Skellig Michael. I thought I'd have some sort of great experience out there. I brought an old chalice with me that I used to use at the Eucharist. I thought I'd take it up to the top of Skellig Michael with all this energy of monks and everything all around me and I'll slip around the corner and feck it into the ocean! Now, that would be a shocking thing to do, but it'd be a ritual to get closure. Get your mother's clothes and give them away to the old folks' home or something, close it. Moving on. And a fella came up, he was out on the boat with me and he was from Russia.

T: Ah, I hate him already!

MH: He was a big fella, he had two women with him. Two women!

T: Bastard!

MH: They were beautiful!

T: Dah, worse again!!

MH: And they kept holding either hand or arm around him on the boat. When they got to the island, one of them said, 'I'm not going up with you, not like that,' and then I realized he was blind drunk. He'd finished a bottle of wine and he had another bottle in his hand. And he went up, and I was racing up the steps in case he'd get ahead of me and put his arm on me, then we'd both go with the chalice. I get to the top, and then he gets up, and there's one of the women beside him but he's pushing her off. He's sitting among the beehives on top of that beautiful place where *Star Wars* and all that craic goes on. The OPW* people tried to calm him and stop him and be gentle with him, and they were brilliant, they were professional.

It's a sheer cliff and the ocean is all around us. Your man is swaying, and he's a big fella. They say, 'Maybe leave the bottle until you're going down, maybe wait until you get down or even wait until you're in the boat, that might be a good idea.' He turned on them, really angry, and he said, 'What did you say? I know what you know, you know fuck nothing, I do what I want.' There's no conversation with him. Talk about a forceful male, right? He went on like that, lecturing them, and they decided to leave him alone, and he came over to me and sat beside me. I didn't want that. I had a paper cup of water and he poured a big dollop of wine into it. I'm sitting there going, 'I'm not going to say I don't want the wine.' Then he said, 'Do you want a sandwich?', so he took out the sandwich and pushed it in my face. I felt it'd be rude to say no! I said, 'Thanks very much.' I'm sitting there on a rock outside one of these beehives with bread and wine. [*Tommy and audience erupt into laughter*] I'm not joking. I said he must be speaking to me now. I swear to God.

T: Wow.

* Office of Public Works.

MH: I ate the sandwich and I didn't drink the thing – I was terrified I'd be dizzy going down. I left the chalice in the bag, I came home, and I said, 'I'd better write down this story.'

T: That's amazing.

MH: So I'm kind of stuck with religion. Other people have other problems in life. I don't think of it as some sort of wisdom . . . All my life I have had this sense of living a mistake. Now this is a true story: there was a fella in a certain city of Ireland, an auld parish priest, and he'd be stressed and have high blood pressure if there was a Communion. This is in Cork, to be telling the whole story. A different parish led the Corpus Christi procession every year, and this fella's turn came and he was terrified. He was going down Patrick's Street with the Guards and the Legion of Mary girls and flowers and petals and choirs. He'd be under the four-poster bed thing and holding the cross with the host in it, and him being there was a really big deal. So he's very stressed, but it all happens well and he's there in the middle of it. A friend came up to him and whispered in his ear, 'We forgot the host.' And your man said, 'Fuck it, we always forget something.' I thought that story is like the way my life has gone. It's been a series of mistakes and forgetting things and not being smart enough for something. That's the way I hold on to religion. It's probably a crutch.

T: That seems like a great gift to me, Michael. There's kind of humanity in it or something.

MH: There might and there mightn't be. I wouldn't say I'm humble.

T: So you're the best worst person ever!

MH: You could be looking at the world like you were the wisest person in the world and the most humble person in the world, and you could have every tattoo in the world talking about how humble you were. Sure I know nothing! We're devious creatures and we never find our centre. We get up in the morning and we tell ourselves this story. We look in the mirror and we say, 'I'm going to cut the grass today, I'm going to do this, that and the other, today.' We tell ourselves a narrative and we say, 'That's who I am.' 'I'm going to talk to that daughter of mine today.' You're telling yourself your story: 'That's who I am.' And you constantly do that, and to some extent prayer is when the stories end. And if you can get to one point of one story or the next and there's literally nothing going on in your head.

T: Would you ever feel guilty about coming across to people as depressed?

MH: Why?

T: Well, you might meet somebody and your energy is low, and you're thinking, I'm not much craic to these people now.

MH: Yeah, I felt that lots of times. I think you get used to it. I always felt melancholic when I was a young fella. All the time I had a melancholy that was natural and normal, but then when it became extreme and I got ill, I thought for a while it wasn't normal. I thought that this melancholy, which now I was calling depression, was not normal, it was an illness. After three or four years of therapy, I realized that depression *is* normal – everybody suffers with it, it's not an illness, it's a point of growth. Depression, when it happens to somebody, is this amazing opportunity of growth, because what's happening is you're letting go of a whole cluster of narratives, a whole cluster you have lived with and woven around you for years. In depression, something breaks them, they can't sustain themselves, they start to fall off you and you feel, this is horrible, this is like death. Because you are letting go of yourself in some sense, the self you've constructed.

T: There's huge insecurities in that.

MH: There's huge insecurities in it, but after that, there's a recognition that that's a growth point. I really do feel that.

T: It's very hard to identify it as that in that space, though. It feels like you're just defeated, you're letting people down, and that you're no craic to be around. And often what causes great conflict then for people is that they might have those feelings but their work, which they're obliged to keep doing in order to keep living in the house they're still living in, forces them to keep the mask on.

MH: One of the most terrible things I felt in depression was the sense that it wouldn't end. It's just a small thing, and yet so huge with people who get depressed. They feel this will never end. If you looked at it from outside, you know it will end, and one of the strongest things I felt that anybody was able to say to me in depression was, 'You'll get out of this.' There's a lovely phrase that you're living in 'the swampland of the soul' when you're depressed. You're going down to embrace that darkness. That's all. I find I have more equanimity and can understand why people say that the older people get, the happier they get. The reason they get happier is because you do accommodate yourself to death. You realize it's OK, it's really natural, a communal process, like a leaf falling off a tree. There's poetry in it.

T: Do you spend much time outdoors?

MH: I spend a lot of time in the garden. I have a garden of trees and I spend a lot of time walking around there, and also walking about Arigna, Arigna Mountain and Lough Allan. I like to pray when I'm walking.

T: So the prayer that you have when you're walking, what is it?

MH: Well, first of all, the human being is spiritual. If we collapse everything into the empirical and rational, we've lost half of what this life is about. Spirituality, somebody defined [it] recently as radical amazement – simply to live with a sense of intense amazement that we're here, because there is nothing more amazing, right? That's prayer – just to be there in that sense of radical amazement. Imagination can really cause trouble, but it also can be your biggest road into being fully human. That's where poetry starts, in metaphors, and where poetry reaches its completion is in 'God', or whatever you want to call it. The journey we're now making in modern countries is to transcend that space where we used to unconsciously get possessed by religion, get possessed by God or demons, and we'd bate the bejaysus out of the other fella because our religion was better than his. Or hers. There's usually him and him.

T: Or bate the bejaysus out of ourselves . . .

MH: . . . for not living up to a dysfunctional idea of spirituality that was full of shame and guilt. But it's hard to use religion well. Buddhism, Islam, Judaism – they're all right and true if they bring us into the present moment and allow us to live here and now. There's that story about an older rabbi meeting a young rabbi who tells him about a big theological idea. The old rabbi says, 'You know, you are right!' And then another young rabbi comes to him and tells the old fella a totally different theological idea. The old rabbi listens, and he says, 'You know, you are right!' God, who has been listening, says to the old rabbi, 'They said totally different things, how can they both be right? They can't.' And the old rabbi says to God, 'You are right too.'

T: That's beautiful. Do you get a sense that the way you spend your days when you're touring with the books and talking to people, that that's a wonderful way to spend time? How does being the storyteller affect you?

MH: I love you. You're amazing, and you have given me moments of insight in the short few times I was privileged to be working with you that have stayed with me. I remember one time we were in the Pavilion in Dún Laoghaire and we were trying to analyse what makes you happy when you're telling jokes, when you're telling the story of sadness and sorrow in the way that makes them human, and you said sometimes when you're with an audience and you're engaging with them, something opens up like that inside of you and you don't know what it is but that it's the most beautiful thing that ever happens to you. I felt that is as clear a sense of prayer as you could ever imagine.

We used to say in the old Catholicism that prayer was an opening of the mind and heart to God. Now we get fixated with the word 'god', but listen to the verb in it; 'an opening of the mind and heart'. There's moments when it happens when you're walking in Arigna on your own by the lake, or in Donegal by the sea, or, I'm sure, at the top of Skellig Michael, when those monks were up there. It happens with love and sex and quiet intensity and the joy of two heads lying on a pillow looking at each other, and having a smoke and saying, 'What did you say your name was?' But you know what I mean. You could be married as long as I am or you are and there's still times on the pillow with the wife looking at you like, 'Who are you?' You know that you can discover the stranger in your partner regularly. But whether it's in love or whether it's you onstage, there's this opening you feel in yourself, and there's no way you can explain that rationally.

You have to use the language of prayer and poetry to say that. It shines out of you when you're on the stage, when you're doing that. You ease people's hearts open to share with you the sadness of human accidents and we all can laugh.

T: People listening to you will be impressed by the feeling you give about 'just whatever works'. How do we encounter ordinary Catholicism in a way that makes it work? It just seems to me that we have a tradition – and, for good reason, we have lost touch with it – but we now maybe have forgotten how to engage with it in a way that is meaningful.

MH: The faith I had when I was a child is the same faith I have now. I say the same prayers and feel the same power of poetry. How do we connect with it? Maybe all this change that is happening, the exposure of stuff from sexual scandals, child abuse, the diminishment of the power and authority of the Church within the state, maybe all these things are blessings. Maybe getting rid of a nineteenth-century authoritarian, all-male Church is not an anti-Church or anti-Christian thing to do. Maybe it's a very deep instinct of 'the spirit', in Catholic terms, saying, 'We need to let go of an awful lot of this, boys, if we want to go back again and hear the meditative silence that you get from Jesus.' It's not rocket science and it's not ecstasy and it's not some sort of hallucination. The 'kingdom of heaven' is being with the other person and putting them ahead of yourself and finding the joy in that. The pure joy you get from a child, or that you get from an audience maybe, the pure joy that you're serving somebody else.

We can easily rediscover the riches that are there in the Christian tradition from the monks of the early Irish Church and all the mystics of Europe. I think it's all there. There's a beautiful text in Buddhism called 'The Heart Suits Her', and the core of 'The Heart Suits Her' is the line that says, 'The ultimate teaching is that there is no teaching.' There's your freedom, there's your enlightenment. It's a step away. You'll find people in the West who have converted to Buddhism, and they'd kind of make you nervous. The grip they have on it, and they'd be telling you about it and they'd be very firm and anxious that you'd washed out all the Catholic nonsense and started meditating properly or whatever. But if you're gripping the teachings, you're missing it, because you have to let your grip loose, let go of everything and just be here now and do whatever is right for you.

T: I just had a fantasy there while you were talking.

MH: Very disappointed in you, Tommy . . .

T: It is all well and good to say, 'Let go of everything,' and 'Whatever works for you,' but some of us need something a bit more practical. While you were talking there, I had this notion of us as a culture and a country that has been through so much in terms of the authority that we have handed over to other people. I had a vision of all of us; we're in a church, there's no priest, there's no ritual, there's no book, there's just us in a church, waiting. And it seemed to me that that would be a fine place for us to start. Put ourselves in that position. No guru, no method, no teacher. Sitting there and waiting, and something would evolve out of that . . . It's always a revelation talking to you, Michael.

Paul McGrath

'I think I've hurt a lot of people along the way,
and I'm just trying to get through my life now hurting
as few as I can, put it that way.'

Tommy: You have some stories to tell.

Paul McGrath: As do you.

T: Yeah, but you've had drama. Obvious, big drama. Will I remind you!? I'm curious about growing up here, the hugeness of your career, the chaos after it, and this moment now. Like, you've had big events in your life.

PM: I have. And I've been blessed with those events. I started this whole thing in an orphanage, and then to come out of that and to be lucky enough to be accepted. There wasn't so many black people around back in those days, so to be accepted by Irish people and to be able to kick a ball, a bag of wind, and get dragged over to Manchester United and stuff like that. I was a very lucky man to have grown up in this country.

T: In fairness now, you were more than accepted by us. You're truly loved by us, and you couldn't put that love down to any one thing. That's the feeling I sense around the country for you. Who ran the orphanage?

PM: I think it was a Protestant orphanage, the first one that I went into, because I was in the Boys Brigade at one stage of my life – they all wear flat hats and stuff like that. I think it's a Protestant thing . . . I didn't know until I showed someone a picture of me in the Boys Brigade. I think it was Norman Whiteside, and he was thinking, how can you be a Catholic? – I became a Catholic later on in life, but I was brought up as a Protestant – and it was simply because my mother didn't want me to grow up in a Catholic situation.

T: Did your mam leave you into the orphanage?

PM: She did. It was, you know, a dodgy sort of time. She dropped me in, and it was, 'See you soon.' My mother was brilliant, you know, she just was. I mean, she started working when she was thirteen, so she had a hard life. I was sent to one or two places, and I loved it, because there was a lot of other people too that I could start soccer matches with where you learn how to play and try to hone my skills.

T: And are you still connected with some of the people that you were in the orphanage with?

PM: Not really, no. They've all done really well, though. I hear from time to time that some of them are ministers. One of them's in the arts sector or something.

T: Do you look back on it as a good time?

PM: I do, yeah . . . Kind of do. Parts of it were bad. There were two places in Dún Laoghaire – one was the Bird's Nest, and then the older boys had to go to Glensilva from the age of ten, and of course there was a lot of big brothers up there that you had to say hello to. They had little brothers down in the Bird's Nest, so they would've been told stories – 'You know the black lad? He hit me.' And the older brothers could be as old as eighteen, so some big guys in there. You had to try and stand your ground. I had the odd row with the older brothers and stuff like that. So that was tough, because I didn't mind a fight but I didn't want to be fighting with people who were a lot older than me.

T: You seem very gentle.

PM: Depends on whatever someone's doing to me, to be honest. I'm gentle with people who are gentle with me. I'm not someone who goes around looking for a fight or anything like that, but you know, I think I did become a little bit of a bully, because that's what happened to me. But I hated being a bully, so when I went up to the other place I was going to change my ways, but I didn't get a chance to, really.

T: How do you spend your time now? What do you do for money?

PM: I love golf. Now, I hated golf when I was a footballer, probably because I couldn't play. I still can't play, but I at least try. If people ask me to do things for charity, I like to try and do that as much as I can. I've been lucky, really, that I still get asked to go to Aston Villa and places like that. They give you a bag of money for talking to people and just being yourself. But I've had to learn how to do that because I'm a shy kind of human being and I don't like even doing *this* – TV! I love it because I'm doing it with you, but I haven't got the face for TV, put it that way.

T: Did you earn a phenomenal amount of money while you were playing? I know it's not as mental as the money now.

PM: No, it wasn't. I was on really low wages at Manchester United, and that's the whole crux of the thing of why I left. Bryan Robson was on a certain amount of money, but you knew Bryan Robson was the best player by far. But I was so far back that the reserve team players were getting more money than me. So I went in to see Sir Alex [Ferguson] and I just said, 'If you could just up my wages a little, that'd be great' – I wasn't good in negotiations – and of course he didn't take kindly to that. He just said, 'What? Up your wages? Get out!' And that's the reason I just thought, well, I can stay here on the same wages for the next five to seven years or I'm going to have to ask to leave. But I didn't really have to ask to leave in the end because Sir Alex did it for me.

T: Was that because yourself, Norman Whiteside and Bryan Robson were fond of a pint?

PM: And Kevin Moran and Gordon McQueen and a few others! Bryan could drink for England, like, he had hollow legs. He could stand at the bar all day. I couldn't. I didn't drink to be social. I just drank because I was afraid of the next thing that was coming around the corner. It was all new to me. But Norman was just a brilliant player as well. A brilliant player. But he did love a couple of pints and stuff, and I just got caught up in it. If someone was having a party in their house, I had to be drunk before I got there, I had to be the one that was starting to be rude to people and getting asked to leave. I didn't like being in people's company for too long, put it that way.

T: What kind of drunk were you? I would think of myself as quite a friendly drunk, you know? A soft eejit drunk.

PM: Would you have bought me a drink then?

T: I'd have been afraid of you! But you didn't like who you were drunk?

PM: No, I wouldn't have. Not at all, because it changed my whole personality. I'm a real quiet sort of person. When I was sitting in a room full of players and someone asks a question, they'd have to shout the question at me and I'd still be trying to hide on them, which is ridiculous. And it was tough, because I just didn't like being in the limelight. The only time I liked being in a football team is when I was on the pitch. The rest of it was hell for me.

T: Did you have a partner during that time?

PM: Ah yeah, I've had a couple of wives. Not at the same . . .

T: Your own, though?

PM: They were my own wives! No, just two, and they were brilliant. They were just magnificent. I've got six kids, and I still talk to both my wives and my kids a lot as well. So it's all worked out and we don't hate each other any more.

T: You seem remarkably self-possessed and in control of things. There's a great calmness coming off you and it's very nice to sit with you. You're very easy.

PM: I don't know where I get that from, because I was panicking like hell about having to sit here and try, and I was thinking, what'll I do, what'll I say? And yeah, it's a lot easier than I thought it'd be, to be honest, because I don't usually like crowds. I'm not used to it.

T: How often do you have to do the talking-in-public thing?

PM: Quite often now, because that's what people ask me to do, to come back to Birmingham and Manchester United, and even Sheffield United sometimes. It is a way to make a living. I have six kids, and I want to be able to buy them stuff. Maybe not as many presents as I used to buy them when they were young. My oldest is thirty-four, so he should start buying his own stuff since he's at that age, shouldn't he?

T: Yeah. And when you do these talks, what do you talk about?

PM: Well, it's usually the same things, like, 'How was it playing against Maradona?' or other players they loved that I might have played against.

T: And what was it like to play Maradona?

PM: It wasn't a happy experience. He did one thing that I just thought was ridiculous. He'd been out with Bryan

Robson the night before, so he was the worse for wear. Someone blasted the ball at him and he just put out his leg, stopped the ball on the end of his toe, and held it there. I was supposed to be marking him, and instead I'm about ten yards away, just looking at him while he kept the ball on his toe, and then he just puts it to the ground and runs off and I'm just thinking, how do you do that? And that's the sort of player he was. He was just a genius.

T: What other famous players would you have played against?

PM: Eric Cantona. Graeme Souness – tough man, hard man. Roberto Baggio as well.

T: Who impressed you the most?

PM: I think Baggio for me, I suppose, because he had a way of getting around you by just chipping the ball all over the place and coming back and getting it off someone and moving it somewhere else. I found it difficult to follow him around the pitch, anyway.

T: What's the greatest compliment that another footballer has paid you?

PM: Andy Gray – I remember I tackled him and actually caught the ball, and he spun up in the air and he landed and he started just giving me elbows. I was only young at Old Trafford then, but he was trying to beat me up. I was thinking, what are you trying to beat me up for? And it was because it was just such a good tackle. I took that as a compliment.

T: When you stopped playing, how chaotic did it get?

PM: Oh, very for me, and everyone was saying, 'What are you going to do when you finish football?' Sure, it was the only thing I ever knew. I wasn't very good at school – I think I was expelled just before I left Sallynoggin. I kind of panicked and I didn't know what I was going to do. But then I was finishing my second divorce, so I just decided that I'd come back to Ireland, find somewhere to live and live a quiet life and just try and be happy.

T: Did you go mad on drink for a while?

PM: Ah yeah, I would've. That was my way of just . . . kind of slamming the gates and just sitting in the house and getting in a bad way. Friends would come and try and get me out of the house, but sure I was a shocking person to try and do anything with when I was drunk because I just didn't like myself and I didn't like what I was doing to my children. I wanted to be a good father to all six of my kids, and I wasn't. That was tough. It's not the only reason, though – I was never very confident, that's what it boils down to.

T: And when you drank – you're drinking by yourself?

PM: Yeah, I drink in the house. I just close the curtains and just sit there and just drink. Lately even started talking to myself . . . I'm getting worried about that side of it now.

T: Did your drinking get dangerous, do you think?

PM: It would have, yeah. I drank anything. You want to get out of your head, and I think a lot of footballers get this when they finish – they face that loneliness that suddenly comes on when you don't have twenty-five players all having the craic with you. You miss that part of the game. I am putting this the wrong way, but I used to love when the match starts and you can actually run up to a player and try and take the ball off him and hit him – at the same time without hurting him, like, but trying to take the ball fairly. I used to think that that was an art. I lived for Saturdays and Sundays – or even Wednesdays, or whenever it was – because I just loved trying to time tackles well.

T: And was it difficult stopping drinking?

PM: It still is. It still is for me. I don't drink half as much as [I used to] . . . I shouldn't say it like that, because that would be quite a lot. But yeah, I do find it hard, and I'd be a liar if I said I've completely stopped drinking. I've cut it down to where it's manageable. I don't drive cars and I don't do the bad things when I'm depressed or drinking or whatever I'm doing. I still try and keep myself to myself, and I get asked to do things from time to time that I really want to do. I'm not trying to blow you up or anything, but when I heard it was you I said, 'I would like to do that.' I think I've hurt a lot of people along the way, and I'm just trying to get through my life now hurting as few as I can, put it that way.

T: I know what you mean. I drank a good bit and then I stopped for ten years, and started back again. It's always that thing of when you start drinking again you know you're aware of the danger of it. But it seems to me like a more mature relationship with alcohol. But you're not saying, 'No, never ever' – you're saying, 'I know it's dangerous but I think I can handle it.'

PM: Therein lies the problem – I think I can. Even when I played football, I've always loved being a little bit on the edge. I'd turn up a little [drunk] a few times or have a few the night before, or have something in my bag, and I'd still go out because I thought that was a dangerous thing to do – play a game [with] even a full glass of whiskey in me. I'd go out then and think, you have to be brilliant today. You have to try and make yourself brilliant today because you're taking the mick out of the rest of the lads. And it didn't always work out.

T: Mostly did, though.

PM: Well, a lot of times.

T: I think you could be on to something! So, all those times we were looking at you going, 'He is amazing – the application, the dedication, the effort.' And you're going around saying: 'God, I'm steamed.'

PM: A lot of times, I was calling for help, though. I was always asking other players, Sean Teale or Dwight Yorke or people like that, for a dig-out,* and that shouldn't be in the soccer game, where someone's saying, 'Can you give me a dig-out this week and I'll help you out next week?' But that's what I was doing, because I was a lunatic.

T: That's interesting, isn't it, the whole thing of looking for the edge?

PM: Yeah, I wasn't taking any drugs that would enhance my [performance]. I had to take just alcohol. It was stupid what I was doing because I was making it easier for the players I was playing against. But then, it would give me some sort of heightened thing where I wanted to stop them.

T: In terms of looking for that edge, has it gone away as you've got older, do you find, or is the public speaking now where that edge is, that risk?

PM: No, I don't have it now. I'm still not good with the public speaking, I wish I was, but I'm just not. People used to say to me, 'Are you going into management?', and I'd just start laughing at them because the thought of me actually standing in a room even of kids and trying to organize them for a match, that would scare the living daylights out of me. So your options get cut down and down and down, and then you have to start worrying about ways that you can actually make money. And so I just do the public speaking, and then there are sometimes other things that I get asked to do that

* Help on the playing field.

are ridiculous, but I do them because it's easy enough for me to do. So I'm lucky. I've always felt blessed that I was taken under the Irish people's wing. I love that I was brought here when I was brought here, at eight weeks old. And I was taken to heart by the Irish people and I can still make a living.

T: Without sounding sentimental or trite, I had a bit of a reaction when you said you were taken 'under the wing' of the Irish people, because I have no sense of that at all. You're Irish. You're as Irish as I am. There's no sense of we're doing *you* a favour. If anything – and I speak for a lot of people – you're the one who did *us* a favour.

Róisín Murphy

'Are you falling in love with me?'

Tommy: I've been reading about you for years. So what I know of you is that you're based in England . . .

    Róisín Murphy: Yes.

    T: And you're . . .

    RM: A woman.

    T: After that, I'm lost! You're a musician.

    RM: I'm a musician. Well, I don't know, I don't feel like a musician. I actually feel more like an eejit. I feel more like 'a concept', or something or other.

    T: What does that mean?

    RM: Well, I didn't start out to be a musician. Somebody said to me today, 'I don't see you as an electronic kind of artist, I see you more as a singer-songwriter.' And I don't see myself as a singer-songwriter. I fell into music by falling in love with a producer. The night that I met him, I gave him a chat-up line – 'Do you like my tight sweater? See how it fits my body.' And he wanted to record it, so I recorded it that night. I had no intention of becoming a singer or anything like that. We fell in love that night – it was really a way of him showing me his 'large studio equipment' immediately. And because he had a big fancy studio and it was the middle of the night, there was no one there.

    T: Were you wild-high that night?

RM: Completely out of my shitbox!

T: On what?

RM: Well, love and music and connectiveness. I was speaking in tongues, basically, and he wanted to record it. That was how it started. I didn't even sing until I signed a record deal. Up till then, I was chatting and talking stupid nonsense and 'concepting'.

T: What were people buying off you when they gave you the record deal? What were they investing in?

RM: I did not know then at all what was going on. I mean, I was very ballsy at nineteen. I'd already been on my own since I was fifteen or sixteen in Manchester. I'd lived three years in Manchester on my own before I got the record deal. My family moved from Arklow to Manchester. We had family connections and then, when I was fifteen, unfortunately my parents had this huge dramatic break-up. I was really into music at that point and ended up making great friendships in Manchester.

T: And what music was happening around there at the time?

RM: Everything. Absolutely everything was happening in Manchester. It was the late 80s or so.

T: Pill country?

RM: You're obsessed with that, aren't you?

T: I'm just trying to get a grip on you.

RM: It wasn't then for me anyway. I was a late starter in all sorts of things, and when I look back on it, it was amazing, the purity of it all, how I didn't get into very much trouble and so on. And I was everywhere, right across the city at a very young age – Moss Side at the PSV, the Hacienda, going to gigs. I was really into just being weird. I didn't want to come back here with my mother, I just wanted to keep going and finding myself. Luckily, the state looked after me. I went to the DHSS

[Department of Health and Social Security] and I told them the situation, and they said, 'OK, here's money we'll give you every week, and the day you turn sixteen you can have your housing benefits.' I stayed with a friend until I was sixteen, and then they gave me a flat around the corner from all my friends and close to my college and they paid for all that for three years. And I'm so grateful for that. So grateful, because I didn't know what I wanted to do. I didn't know what I was.

T: So late 80s into the 90s – it's all the dance scene in Manchester. It's probably the start of the whole Oasis thing as well, isn't it?

RM: No, that was a bit after it. Actually, I'd already gone to Sheffield when I was nineteen, which is where I started making music with this guy, Mark Brydon. I thought I would be a visual artist since I was around six. My family are extremely funny, interesting people, and I always wanted to know what they were interested in, the music and films that they love, the books my Ma reads. She was an antique dealer so she taught me a lot about stuff, and me Da's a fantastic singer. I come from a very musical background and I'm just lucky I grew up when I did in the place that I did. There wasn't any disconnect.

T: You seem really self-assured. And any time I come across you in the press, you seem so confident and totally in charge of the wildness of your creativity.

RM: Well, I think that's the upbringing as well. Obviously, I must have had that confidence then to make that decision to stay in Manchester. I could have come back here with me Ma. And that moment of making that decision set me as strong and decisive in the eyes of other people as well. That's been good. And that's been bad.

T: I would associate Manchester with a kind of self-possessed toughness, unlike Liverpool, which I think is quite a sentimental city. Manchester seems to me to be able to produce people like you.

RM: Manchester's very sentimental. It's a deeply, deeply sentimental place, with lots of civic pride. Have you seen [Michael Winterbottom's 2002 film] *24 Hour Party People*?

T: Years ago.

RM: Its depiction of Manchester is so true, the combination of that history and then the diversity as it became a more modern city. It's a great place. But Sheffield was even more formative [for me], with the kind of music that came out of there, from The Human League to Cabaret Voltaire to Pulp. Everyone I knew in Manchester was obsessed with music. And as soon as I went to Sheffield, everyone was making music, either the music itself or the album sleeves, or running labels or record shops or clubs, or DJing. It was only a matter of time until I bumped into somebody.

T: What type of music do you make?

RM: Well, I've made music that you can describe as 'dance music' or 'electronic' or 'electronic pop'. And I have made music that you don't know what the hell it is.

T: Sometimes people who are half English, half Irish have a 'tension' – do you?

RM: I'm not half English. There might be a quarter, an eighth or a sixteenth, but I'm not allowed to talk about that!

T: Was it a soldier?

RM: Well, me Da's like the most Irish man in Ireland. His mother is English. That's the only English there.

T: So were you born in Arklow?

RM: Dublin. Then I was reared in Arklow until I was twelve.

T: What I mean is that I encounter it more with people

who, say, lived in Manchester from when they were twelve and then moved to Mayo. A slight kind of, 'I don't really fit in here.' You're someone who has gone the other way and I'm just asking did that create an 'edge' in you in Manchester?

RM: No. Manchester was such a diverse place at that point. I never fitted in anywhere, so that's the first thing anyway. I didn't fit in in Arklow, I didn't fit in in school . . .

T: Why not?

RM: Too full of myself.

T: In a bad way?

RM: I don't think so.

T: Would there be reports sent home?

RM: The teachers didn't like me. The children didn't like me . . .

T: What did the teachers say about you?

RM: That I was naughty, I wasn't behaving well. I was only good at two things in school: camogie and art. That was it. I sang to get into the choir and didn't get in.

T: Why would they not let you into the choir?

RM: She didn't like me, the teacher. In fairness!

T: Were you hyper in class?

RM: No, I'm not hyperactive, I don't think, but dyslexic for sure. But I was very confident because of the way I was brought up, confidence in a certain kind of way. Obviously, we all have our insecurities, but I had a kind of 'I don't care what you think.' I came from an irreligious family. Even now, I'm trying to backtrack a little bit from the way that I was brought up against religion.

T: One of the only children in the country not allowed to go to Mass!

RM: You would go into school and one of the teachers would come around to all the classes and say, 'Everyone who was at Mass yesterday, put up their hands.' And of course, I would always put up my hand, and then she'd go, 'Róisín Murphy! What was the sermon all about then?' And I wouldn't know because I wasn't there, and I'd be in trouble. And I'd say, 'But my parents don't go to Mass,' and she'd say that didn't matter at all. You were expected to go.

T: Did you make your Confirmation?

RM: Yeah, I did all that. Sure you do all that, don't you . . .

T: What name did you take for Confirmation?

RM: I wanted to take Madonna, but they wouldn't let me! It was Joan . . . Collins!

T: Of Arc, perhaps!

RM: I say all this, but now I've got a ten-year-old daughter and she is starting to get interested in boys and all this kind of stuff, and you sort of go, 'You know, you can't do that.' And she goes, 'Why?' And you can't say why because, if you start to say why to a ten-year-old, where are you going to go with that? That's a dark place to go. So you want to be able to say, 'Because you'll go to hell!'

T: Hang on, she's ten! What does she want to do, for God's sake?

RM: You know, she likes this boy and this boy likes her, and it was Valentine's Day and they had the Valentine's exchange and all that . . .

T: Isn't there a marvellous innocence in all that?

RM: Well, I'd like to keep it as innocent as possible! I'd like her to realize that she's going to go to hell until she gets a bit of sense at least!

T: Wow – scary Irish mam! And so the teachers didn't like you because you were dyslexic and there was no manners on you.

RM: They didn't know I was dyslexic. Nobody knew

anybody was bloody dyslexic then. But I got into loads of trouble. I would always get into fights, but I never would win them . . . because I'm so pretty!

T: Not the face, not the face! And why didn't the other students like you?

RM: I don't know. Some of them did like me, for God's sake. But I did get a lot of bullying for being a big-mouth, being maybe insensitive, being full of myself generally, and getting into fights but not able to pull hair out as quickly as I probably should have. I didn't see it as bullying – I just see it as character-building.

T: Jesus, God help your kids! No boys, and take a slap when it's coming!

RM: I think it was my brother said, 'Would you be OK if they went off at fifteen or sixteen like you did?', and you'd have to think for a minute, but it would be amazing for them, you know? It was the best thing I ever did.

T: But does your ten-year-old daughter know that you did that?

RM: No. They're not being drilled with any of that yet!

T: The day they find that out now, that Mammy lived on her own when she was fifteen . . . Good luck with the next argument! Who else was in the family home?

RM: I have a brother, Sean, and he's lovely. Lots of cousins and me Nana, a heavy matriarch. My auntie Linda, my uncle Jim, who was a multi-instrumentalist bandleader and singer-songwriter who loved jazz. I was brought up around a lot of live music. He was pitch perfect. He was amazing, my uncle Jim, and quite famous in his day.

T: In Arklow?

RM: All over. In the summertime, we'd have him do all-day jazz sessions, and I'd be there from the age of five, dancing all day long. I always say that growing up in Ireland at that time was a bit like being in an MGM musical. Everyone just burst out into song every five minutes of the day. Everybody had one, two, ten songs they knew from start to finish that, over the years, kind of merged with their personalities and life stories. So without having to be a stage-school brat or obsessed with fame or anything like that, music at that time in Ireland was just absolutely everywhere. It went in, obviously, but I'm really proud that I discovered it naturally.

T: Do you feel very free when it comes to creating?

RM: No, it's not that feeling, it's a feeling of dedication. You have to have a discipline and you have to feel that you won't be doing anything good unless you feel like you're going to fail.

T: Stressful, though.

RM: But very, very joyful when it comes together.

T: I've noticed a cycle with my life in that I almost volunteer for stressful situations. And I sometimes wonder is the stress the price you pay for the relief you get after the creative act?

RM: If it's easy, if it feels like just a walk in the park, it's not really worth doing. Obviously, when you're performing and you get to a flow state, that's an exquisite moment which perhaps doesn't last as long as it should. But I don't even notice my stress. Only other people are like, 'You're really stressed.'

T: So in terms of, say, creating the next album, what would you say to yourself?

RM: It's not that straightforward. I have so many interests, fleeting ones and deeper ones. Sometimes, I can wake up in the morning and think, I just really want to investigate

70s wrestling in England, and I'll spend six hours looking at videos of that. It's a balance of input and output, or I'd go mad.

T: Do you sell well?

RM: Not particularly. I sell. I've done well. I've had a great career. It's been an unfolding thing over the years and I've made plenty of money, but I'm not famous and I'm sort of proud of that too. When my kids ask me am I famous, that kind of thing, then I'm able to say, 'No, I'm just very well thought of.' I'm respected – to be able to say that in some way and for it to be true . . .

T: Do you still earn then mainly from gigging?

RM: Yeah, the live thing is the best part of it for the money. It's been great the last ten or fifteen years because of all these festivals, so that keeps us all going.

T: Have I seen you connected with the fashion world? Have I seen you photographed wearing, like, staplers . . .

RM: That's next week. I've done all sorts. Yeah, I like clothes. I'm an exhibitionist. It's another thing I've been since a child. I used to dress up in me auntie Linda's 60s wedding dress and her beauty-queen gear, because they were all beauty queens, weren't they, in the old days, and her tiaras and everything. You would swan around Arklow. In Arklow, I used to dress as a Chinese woman and sit in the window of our house on the old Dublin road when all the tourists used to come down in the summer, and I'd open the sash window, put all these naked dolls around me like cherubs and wave at them all as they're going by! 'Mammy, Mammy, look at that eejit up there.' And me Ma brought home this Victorian pram one time – she was an antique dealer, you know – and I dressed up as a Victorian ghost wheeling the pram around. So yeah, an exhibitionist for sure.

T: It's a joy in your own self, isn't it? As in kind of like, 'I'm going to play now.'

RM: It's not just your own self. It's everything. It's a joy in finding stuff. I was primed for that with the way that I was brought up. Me Da could bring anyone home, like some mad auld poet or whoever. I'm really good at throwing people out because I saw me mother doing it so many times. But then this decision that I made in Manchester was really based on a kind of cultural joy I was having, just finding myself and getting into things. When I look back on it, it carried me across a great many dangers. I sort of floated around with this vision of, like, 'That's gorgeous ... that's brilliant music ... that's a great film ... that's a beautiful book ...' And that's all I would really want for my children, that they have interests. That's the point A in which you start to make your own life.

T: Yeah, but it's the question of risk, though, as well.

RM: But there's no decision now without risk. There's no job without risk. There's no anything without risk these days. We're 'post' that. There's no paternalism any more from anywhere.

T: What do you mean by paternalism?

RM: The state will not look after you. You're not going to be able to float. It's sad. You know, it's true. But I've forgotten what we were talking about. What were we talking about?

T: Iraq.

RM: That was bad. That was queer bad, wasn't it? So are you falling in love with me?

T: No, sorry about that. If I don't fall in love with you, maybe we can be friends, you see. Don't get annoyed with me now for that!

RM: The way you look at people, though ...

T: I guess I would sense in myself that I carry a lot of doubt, and I'm always intrigued by confidence.

RM: I carry a lot of doubt. You must have the confidence too. Look at where you are. This is just, like, disingenuous to say you're not confident. You are confident. You're here, right?

T: Yeah.

RM: There is nothing any good without tension. So you've got to have the yin and the yang. What you were you saying about me before – that you're not confident but I am . . .

T: Well, any time I encounter you in the press, you do seem to exude confidence. Just the stories that you've been telling us about growing up and moving to Manchester, you sound just like a child and a young woman who just was determined to fly, irrespective of the space that you were in. And I think that's remarkable.

RM: I carry *a lot* of doubt. It wasn't a big, ambitious thing. It was really just sort of incremental – let's just get into this band, let's just go to that club, let's just meet these people, let's just read that book . . . It's not been some sort of all-singing, all-tap-dancing thing.

T: Do you have lots of friends?

RM: No, I don't have lots and lots, I'm not one of these people like me manager back there. Everybody loves her, it drives me mad! No, I'm not like that. I have friends that I've had since I was fourteen.

T: You mentioned earlier about trying to go back a little bit in terms of religion, being maybe not as strictly against it as your parents were. What did you mean by that?

RM: I can at least threaten the children with hell! I mean, it's just not a big deal. I'm not religious, but I'm not totally frightened of it either. My partner is Italian, and I do like the pomp of Catholicism, and I like the art that came out of it and the architecture that came out of it. And I do see that some good things, some fantastic things, came out of it.

T: My own father said to me one time, he said, 'Religion is fine, Tom, just don't think too much about it.'

RM: Or talk too much about it.

T: I was in Venice – last year, I think – and myself and my wife went into this beautiful old Italian church, and they're just places of beauty and comfort without having to come up with a belief system that justifies it.

RM: Absolutely.

T: Just to recognize this is good. This is nice.

Acknowledgements

Much love, admiration, respect and gratitude to the production team who put the show together: David Power, Therese Kelly, Olive Esler, Kate O'Dwyer and, from Series 1, Nicola Bardon. They do six months of work before it even starts.

Thanks also to the editors who have worked with us so far: Edmund Slattery (Series 1), Ultan Murphy (Series 2), John Murphy (Series 3) and Jim Dalton (Series 4). And the directors: Alan Byrne (Series 1) and Maurice Linnane (Series 2, 3 and 4).

Thanks to my Gussett Brothers – John Colleary and Pat McDonnell – and my MCs for the evening, the beautiful Mr Fred Cooke and, for Series 3, Julie Jay.

Special thanks to all the helpful souls in RTÉ who gave me such encouragement and the funding to be able to do the show: Adrian Lynch, Eddie Doyle, Justin Healy. Also Dan Healy in 2FM, who gave us the chance to do the show on radio as a start. Marcella in production design and the RTÉ studio crew in general have been great to work with. Thanks to Triona Lillis for dressing me in the most wonderful clothes and Michelle Kinsella for my make-up.

Huge thanks to Michael McLoughlin and Patricia Deevy from Sandycove for their patience, wisdom and attention to detail. And thanks to Hilary White for great work editing the transcripts.

Thanks to my manager, Caroline Chignell, and Patrick

Bustin at PBJ, without whose wisdom, care and skill I'd be floundering.

Big love to my family:

My wife, Yvonne.

My children – Dylan, Jake, Eve, Isobel, Louis and Theo.

And my granddaughter, Ava.